To My Friend Mo

With Best wishes

Love

from

Allan

*the*

LONG MARCH

*of the*

# Market Men

*the*
# LONG MARCH
*of the*
# Market Men

# ALLAN STEWART
with Harry Conroy

**A**rgyll
publishing

First published in 1996 by
Argyll Publishing
Glendaruel
Argyll PA22 3AE
Scotland

**British Library Cataloguing-in-Publication Data.**
**A catalogue record for this book is available from the**
**British Library.**

ISBN 1 874640 57 2

*Origination*
Cordfall Ltd, Glasgow

*Printing*
Bookcraft (Bath) Ltd

*To*
Susie

ACKNOWLEDGEMENTS

I would like to thank all those who have helped me in the preparation of this book – first and foremost, Harry Conroy who has been the main force behind the writing and who by a combination of hard work, charm and persistent bulldozing has coaxed the final text from me; Derek Rodger, the publisher, who has had the faith (at times sorely tested) to believe that the manuscript in its entirety would actually be delivered; to Douglas Mason for his constructive contributions and calming influence; to Jeanette Muir for typing parts of the text; to the House of Commons Library for their excellent service; and to my family for their forbearance and encouragement.

I acknowledge with gratitude also all those constituency office bearers, executive and party members and friends whose hard work and support make it such a privilege to serve as Member of Parliament for Eastwood.

Finally, I thank my parliamentary colleagues and opponents who have made the past seventeen years at Westminster the most facinating, challenging and enjoyable of my life so far.

Allan Stewart
March 1996

CONTENTS

I had no ambition to enter politics when I arrived at St Andrews University in 1960. I had chosen Political Economy for my degree course because it represented to my mind a practical approach to economics. I embarked on my higher education with no particular political slant in mind.

Neither was there any precise date when I suddenly embraced a political philosophy. In my early years at university I confined myself largely to student politics.

The Political Economy department of St Andrews was at that time a stronghold of the principles of a free market economy under the guidance of Professor James Wilkie Nisbet and had previously featured Ralph Harris, now Lord Harris of High Cross and a doyen of Britain's market economy thinkers.

In the early sixties proponents of the free market were looked upon with some suspicion and Keynesian economics still held sway. There was no doubt that St Andrews University's Political Economy department was approaching the subject from a more open standpoint than other universities at that time.

This did not mean that as a student you had to accept the views being put forward within the department. Many of the students of that time held firmly to Keynes, but personally I increasingly accepted the free market views I heard being promulgated by Professor Nisbet and members of his staff, including those of Bob Schuettinger, an American visiting lecturer who is now a Professor at Oxford University.

Bob Schuettinger wrote a powerful booklet attacking Government policies on prices and incomes in the late sixties.

I became a close friend of Bob's. He was an intellectual, and stood for the Senate in the United States as a Republican. He was drafted into the US Navy where they identified him as having the lowest possible mechanical aptitude, a description which I can easily accept.

I can recall visiting his flat once and noticed that his desk, which was always covered in papers, had been moved. I asked him why he had moved the desk and he explained that the light bulb which shone over where the desk had previously been situated no longer worked.

I suggested that it would have been easier if he had just changed the bulb, and he replied, "I don't know how to do that." Bob may not have known how to change a light bulb, but as a free market economist he was very influential.

His booklet on prices and incomes policy showed that governments had tried this method of controlling the economy for 2000 years right back to the time of the Roman Empire, and it had not worked.

This widespread belief, prevalent at that time, in a prices and incomes policy has disappeared. As a Government method of controlling the economy it simply has not worked and it is one of the major victories of the free market principles espoused by Bob and other economists at St Andrews that this economic theory is no longer credible.

None of the major political parties now advocate prices and incomes as one of their planks concerning the economy yet both the Heath and Callaghan governments in the 1970s tried it.

Until this period St Andrews had no track record of producing politicians. In Scotland this had been more the province of universities such as Glasgow. However the free market philosophy developed in St Andrews was to spawn a number of political personages including Michael Forsyth the Secretary of State for Scotland.

There is no doubt in my mind that the lectures in Political Economy being given in St Andrews at that time were to influence many far beyond the confines of the university lecture rooms. Ralph Harris when he left the university went on to found the Institute of Economic Affairs and his views underpinned the intellectual force behind Margaret Thatcher's policies as Prime Minister.

The free market philosophy which emanated from St Andrews did influence events and decisions between 1978 and 1983. I can recall Keith Joseph visiting East Renfrewshire after I had been adopted as a prospective candidate, and I gave him a lift in my car to Glasgow Central station.

It had been a long day for him and he was quiet as we drove in. To be polite he asked me which university I had gone to, and when I said St Andrews he immediately perked up and said – "That's where it all happened." The free market principles I adopted during my times at St Andrews are still with me to this day, but the contrast is they are now very widely accepted.

They are that the State sets the basic framework and that although there are some activities only the State can reasonably carry out such as defence, the balance of the economic argument is to allow individuals to do what they want to do, with the minimum interference from Government.

This leads to diversification of power which is good for democracy. History shows a country can have a market economy without democracy but not democracy without the market.

The market is a more efficient mechanism than Government controls. If people pursue their own interests within the framework of the law that will in overall terms be in the general interest.

Market forces create a political dynamism of their own but I do not argue for a laissez faire type of society. I have never taken the view that anything goes. This is a dangerous position for supporters of the free market to take.

Markets are seldom perfect and can impose what economists call disexternalities. If an activity creates a social cost governments should use the price mechanism to ensure that the producer pays.

In the sphere of controlling environmental damage, for example, I take the view that the polluter should pay. Rather than introducing State controls on such activity, the Government should impose a tax on the producer. VAT on fuel is an example of this principle being applied when the Government had to take action to reduce sulphur dioxide in the atmosphere.

It is the belief in the market which has guided me through my political career. When I first espoused it in St Andrews in the 1960s there were many people who thought we were economic cranks, and few politicians of any standing gave credence to our views.

One of the exceptions was Enoch Powell who, when he was a Tory MP, was a strong supporter of the free market and it was for this reason that he became the President of the St Andrews Conservative Association, a contributor to its magazine and speaker at its centenary dinner.

The influence of those holding these minority views have extended into the heart of political economic thinking through people such as Madsen Pirie, founder of the Adam Smith Institute and Douglas Mason while Lord Harris continued to argue for the free market via the Institute of Economic Affairs after leaving the north east corner of Fife to take his views into the heart of Whitehall.

This background will perhaps allow the reader to put into context the arguments I put forward in the late 60s and early 70s for independent commercial radio and student loans which at the time were considered to be slightly eccentric but which are now widely accepted as sensible policies which few people question.

It has indeed been a Long March for the Market Men, but we have come a long way in the thirty or so years covered by this book, and we are not at the end of the road yet.

CHAPTER 1

# THE EARLY YEARS

I had a secure childhood being brought up in the quiet country town of Cupar in Fife. Born on June 1, 1942, I was a war child and like many other young children who came into the world at that time I did not see my father until he returned from fighting in the war.

I was three and a half then and my mother had always shown me photographs of my father. She told me later how she was worried about how I would react when I first saw him, but as it turned out there was not a problem. After my father came into the house I toddled over to his photograph and told my mother, "I have two Daddies now."

My father, Edward MacPherson Stewart was in the RAF

during the war attached to a radar unit. He fought in Africa, then up through Italy. At the end of hostilities he returned to teaching English in Dundee High School where he eventually became Rector. Before the war he had also taught in Dundee at Morgan Academy. He met my mother Eadie Barrie Stewart while teaching in Morgan Academy where she had been secretary to the Rector. Despite sharing a common surname they were not related.

I was christened John Allan Stewart, but I have always been called Allan, and never John. This was probably because there were so many other Johns in the family – my maternal grandfather was also called John. I can remember my paternal grandfather whom I was called after opening one of my books when I was eight or nine. I had signed my name as Allan Stewart, and he asked me what was wrong with my first name, and told me never to forget my first name. This is why I always sign myself as J Allan Stewart. The Allan was my paternal grandmother's name.

My upbringing was, I suppose, typical middle class. In Cupar we lived in an attractive detached house called Glenelg off Balgarvie Road. It was an unused lane with no passing traffic. The house had a small garden back and front with a high wall at the back beyond which was Duffus Park. There was a tennis club and putting area in the park and a little corner shop nearby.

My mother and father had first lived in Wick after they were married, but when my father went off to the war my mother moved to Cupar to live with her father. He had owned a plumbing business in Cupar and to this day you can still see manholes with the name Stewart on them.

After the war, when my father returned home, we continued to live in the family house in Cupar. Every day my father would cycle to the railway station to catch a train to Dundee. I attended the local Castlehill Primary School. I was followed by my young sister Kathleen, who was born in 1946 as one of the post-war baby boom. Kathleen is now a corporate lawyer in Edinburgh.

Summer holidays were normally taken in Upper Largo or Carnoustie where my paternal grandfather had a house. We would also occasionally travel as far as Montrose where my father's sister

Mary lived with her husband, Rev James Wilson, who was a minister. Kathleen and I would stay in the manse. We were very fortunate in those days to take seaside holidays with the family.

Cupar was the county town of Fife and life in it was conducted at a sedate pace. The town's architecture is mainly Georgian and Victorian with the striking Corn Exchange tower which was built in 1861.

Our family life reflected the town. I was a member of the Lifeboys, and I appeared in the school plays, and as I grew older was in the church dramatic club. My parents both attended the local Bonnygate Church of Scotland where my mother's family had a pew. Father was an elder of the kirk and my mother was also active in church and increasingly Red Cross affairs.

After the primary years my sister and I both went to Bell Baxter High School which was truly a comprehensive and served the entire community. I was encouraged to study, which is not surprising with my father being a teacher, and my academic performance improved as I went through school. Before I left I was school captain and Dux of the school. In fifth year I gained Highers in English, Maths, History, French and Latin. I also passed German and Arithmetic at the lower level.

My academic performance may have improved as I got older, but I cannot say the same for my sporting achievements although I represented the school at athletics, rugby and golf. However I decided I was never going to be an athlete after I came in fifth in a mile race at least 100 yards behind the winner, and half an hour later was still lying flat out, totally exhausted.

I captained the school's second fifteen rugby team, and although I enjoyed the game I was not particularly good at it. My father was a member of Cupar Golf Club which I joined when I was around nine years old. I would often cycle down to the club for a game which I played well but not brilliantly. By the time I was seventeen my handicap was 12. Though opportunities to play are rare, today I am a member of the Caldwell Golf Club in Uplawmoor.

After gaining my Highers in fifth year I stayed on for a sixth, and sat numerous scholarship exams for St Andrews University which is the university that my father had attended. I gained a Ramsay residential scholarship and two small bursaries which helped to pay my way through university. The Ramsay is not one of the better known scholarships and when I told my father I had gained a scholarship he immediately told me, "I know, it is the Ramsay." I was taken aback and asked him how he knew. He simply said, "I dreamt it." There is a tradition of second sight in my father's family, although I do not personally claim to have it.

At St Andrews University I was allocated a single room in St Regulus Hall. My best subjects at school had been history and English but I wanted to take a practical degree so I studied Political Economy and Modern History. I had no idea what I wanted do with my future.

Life at St Andrews was very pleasant. I have to admit that I did not study very hard during terms, but instead joined in the student social life. I had several girlfriends and met my future wife Susie while I was at St Andrews. As students we were just acquaintances rather than particularly close friends.

I had been in the debating society at Bell Baxter and had won several prizes in debating competitions while at school. I joined the debating society at university, and although the debates were not political I became involved in student politics which was eventually to lead me into my present career.

Money was not in plentiful supply at university, but we still had a good social life with everything revolving round the university. We would drink coffee and just chat. I don't recall for example, ever going out for a meal during my time there.

I also played golf for the St Salvator's College, in effect the university second team. Students were able to play the Old Course at reduced rates and we had many games over the championship course.

It was a wonderful place and time. The summer at the end of my first year I spent on the continent with a friend, John Todd from the university who had grown up with me; we had gone to Bell Baxter together.

22

We hitch hiked all over Europe right down to Greece. We visited Copenhagen and Paris and travelled through Italy. It was a great holiday, and was the first time I had been abroad. Needless to say we wore kilts.

When I was growing up in Cupar it was very unusual for someone to go abroad for their holidays. My mother was in her sixties before her first foreign holiday when she went with us to Minorca.

To eke out my scholarships I also took summer jobs, and can remember one in particular at a Territorial Army camp at Fort George. It was the year that Aberdeen was virtually cordoned off because of the typhoid scare. The TA normally relied on Aberdeen for their labour to maintain the site doing mainly menial jobs. There were five or six of us from the university including one chap who was training to be a Church of England vicar. He became our 'industrial leader' and negotiated a wage increase for us.

One of the jobs we had to do was to clean the drains. If you did this on a Saturday you were paid one and a half times the rate, but if it was on a Sunday the pay was double time. One Saturday we blocked the drains so that we could clear them on the Sunday and get paid double time!

St Andrews was never lonely. For a start several of my school friends from Bell Baxter such as Derek Barrie had joined me there. I had no lack of friends. People such as Willis Pickard, now editor of the *Times Educational Supplement*, Ronnie Dundas, Financial Editor of *The Herald* and Ewan Brown of Noble Grossart, the merchant bankers were all there at the same time as myself.

St Andrews had the big advantage over some other universities of being a fairly small community. There were tens not hundreds in each class and you soon got to know people.

It was like living in a village with all the advantages of a much bigger town.

When I went up to university I considered myself a Conservative, but I did not have strongly held views. My parents I knew voted National Liberal, but they were not members of the party. They merely exercised their vote and supported the

National Liberal MP for East Fife, Henderson Stuart.

No political figures came around our home in Cupar. Indeed my first contact with a political activist was with a Labour canvasser who knocked on our door. I was about 16 at the time and I just told him that my parents were out.

Many students joined the various political clubs at St Andrews and I joined both the Liberal Club and the Conservative Club. I didn't join the Labour Club simply because there were too many people around their stall when I went along to the pre-term fair which is run every year for new students.

The main reason I joined the Conservatives was that it had a good reputation for having parties and appeared to have a lot of attractive young women as members. Few of the members were really active Tories.

As it happened I didn't remain in the Conservative Club for long. I had the misfortune to meet this rather large gentlemen at one of the first gatherings. He asked me were I came from, and when I replied Cupar, he snorted, "I hope you pass your exams, few of them do." That episode rather put me off the Conservative Club and I didn't return to their meetings.

I began to lean towards the Liberals when James Davie became my senior man. This is a tradition which goes back hundreds of years at St Andrews. Every first year student chooses a third or fourth year student who acts as their mentor. It is a social role and your senior man introduces the first year student (bejant) to people, gives the first year student hopefully useful advice and takes him along to meetings. The practice means that a first year student quickly becomes integrated into university life. During the year on 'Raisin Monday' you give your senior man a pound of raisins, or more likely the fermented or distilled equivalent, and in return he gives you a parchment which is usually insulting in tone. I still have mine, which is written in Latin in ornate script, hanging in my hall. It is a very fine looking document, an outstanding example of a centuries old but still useful University tradition. James later served another useful purpose in my life by hosting the party in London where I met Susie again almost a decade later.

My senior man and Willis Pickard, who was vice chairman of the Liberal Association at the University, both had rooms opposite me in St Regulus Hall, and they were both Liberals.

I became more involved with the Liberal Club and within a year I was the vice chairman. Willis Pickard suggested that I should stand for the Students' Representative Council, telling me that I would get the St Regulus vote.

Douglas Mason, who was later to become a great friend, was my opponent, and as St Regulus was a larger residence than his, I was elected.

At the same time as all this was going on Norman Shanks who was also in St Regulus was standing for the Students' Union in a separate election. Norman also won and he of course went on to become a senior civil servant and was private secretary to Willie Ross at the Scottish Office before joining the Ministry.

He became chair of the Church of Scotland's Church and Nation Committee, and was active in the Scottish Constitutional Convention, the Labour Party dominated body aimed at creating a Scottish Parliament within the United Kingdom. This has led me to crossing swords with Norman on occasion, but no one can doubt the sincerity of his beliefs. What impressed all his fellow students was the simple fact that he always was so well organised. He finished work at 9pm every evening, which was about the time some others of us were starting. No one was surprised that Norman was the top first class honours degree in Arts in his year.

I was 20 and in my second year at St Andrews when I was elected to the SRC. It was not a party political body and concerned itself more with internal student affairs.

I was elected SRC President in my third year and this meant that I had to attend many meetings with the university Principal, Dr Malcolm Knox, who had a poor reputation among the students of whom he was suspected not to be overly fond. However official dealings with him were perfectly amicable.

During this period the writer, C P Snow was elected our Rector. I had supported his campaign and this almost landed me in trouble with the university authorities when I was nearly caught by the porters fly posting. We escaped because I had the keys to the SRC room and we hid in there while they searched the corridors looking for the culprits.

C P Snow was a significant Rector. He believed in bridging the gap between Arts and Science, which was later to become an important educational and political theme.

St Andrews was very pleasant at that time. Every Sunday after morning service we would walk down the pier wearing our distinctive red gowns. We wore the gowns in a different manner depending on which year you were in. If you were in first year you had your gown right up covering both shoulders. In second year, the gown would only cover one shoulder and so on. It meant students and staff could tell which year a person was in simply by the way in which they wore their gown.

It was a beautiful walk and after the residence balls in June we would walk along on the piers in the early hours of the morning and see the sun come up across the horizon out at sea.

My studies were assisted by my good fortune to have excellent Professors and lecturers. The Modern History department was led by the very eminent Namierite, Professor Norman Gash, who specialised in Robert Peel, while the Chair of Political Economy was held by Professor James Wilkie Nisbet who was a critic of the then fashionable neo-Keynesian school of thought. He took a keen, and benevolent interest in his students, and our future.

University staff suggested that I consider academic life as a future career and this idea began to take root as I specialised in Economic History, particularly the link between Political Economy and American History which I found fascinating. It was completely different from European history and I decided then that if the chance arose I would visit the United States.

The opportunity did present itself as I neared the end of my studies at St Andrews. One of my relatives, George Storrar, a farmer, suggested that I apply for a Rotary International Foundation Fellowship. My local Rotary in Cupar nominated me to the North East of Scotland District and I was awarded the

Fellowship. I applied to the Graduate School of Arts and Services at Harvard although without much hope of gaining a place. To my surprise everything went very smoothly and I gained an exchange student place there for a year.

I travelled to Harvard on the *Queen Elizabeth*, and arrived safely at my student abode, Perkins Hall, Oxford Street, Cambridge which struck me as a quintessentially English address.

Despite the familiarity of the address, Harvard was a considerable culture shock. I shared a bedroom and a large study with a fellow student, Norman Brenner, a tall, bearded, amiable New York Jew. Although at first I felt he was somewhat monosyllabic, I later discovered that his initial shortage of conversation was due to the fact that for the first three or four weeks he had not understood a word I said as strong Scottish accents are not common in Brooklyn.

My introduction to American culture came when Norman suggested that we instal a phone in our room. The only phones in the student residences in St Andrews had been the public ones in the common rooms, and even today I would not think that this has altered to any great extent.

I was so taken aback by the suggestion that I enquired what he meant in case I had misunderstood him. Norman explained that the (private sector) telephone company was keen to acquire new customers. The rent was low, and local calls were free, so the telephone was duly installed.

American education I discovered was different from what I had experienced. A huge proportion of the population went on to higher education but generally with lower qualifications than were necessary to enter a Scottish university. My Master of Arts degree from St Andrews was considered a second degree in America.

At Harvard I took a variety of courses in politics and economics, some at postgraduate level and others at under-graduate level. I was not studying for any specific degree but nevertheless sat examinations in the normal way.

We had a TV in our room which meant that I was able to watch the 1964 British General Election results which I found a frustrating experience – not because of the result, but because of the way the results were reported. American viewers were given no indication as to what was happening in terms of the swing from the Conservatives to Labour. The TV stations simply showed the seats being won as the results came in which meant that Labour piled up an early lead as inner city seats then were counted much faster than country seats. This gave no idea of the overall trend.

There were also elections in the United States during 1964. I attended local meetings of both Republican and Democratic candidates including a Barry Goldwater meeting in Boston.

It became very clear that the Americans had a different approach to politics than we do. Voters would not vote strictly along party lines. Many would vote Republican at one level, and for the Democrats at another. This was illustrated by the fact that while Massachusetts voted Democrat in the Presidential elections, Ed Brooke, a Republican was the sitting senator for Massachusetts and held on to his seat.

It was also obvious from the swathe of advertising hoardings that money played a large part in American politics. It was clearly impossible to run for a major office without access to massive amounts of money.

Being on a Rotary International Foundation Fellowship meant that I attended and spoke at Rotary Clubs and I met many individual Rotarians who were extremely kind. I spent a weekend with one who ran a hardware store and appeared to be a very successful business man. But my canny Cupar upbringing meant that I was shocked when he told me that he had gone bankrupt twice.

In Cupar this would have brought disapproval from the local community but the American culture is very different. My Rotarian friend simply explained that even if you lost all your money you are still the same person and your children still attended the same schools. You simply had to pick yourself up and get on with life – a very different attitude from the one which still prevails in Britain today where financial failure is somehow looked upon as something to be permanently ashamed of, rather than an experience on which someone can build.

My Rotary connections meant that during my year at Harvard I went to the Rotary Conference in the Grand Bahama Island which was British territory. The trip led me to experience how strict the Americans are about allowing anyone into their country. Returning from Grand Bahama I came up against the US immigration authorities. Their attitude appeared to be that while I wasn't a proven drug dealer, I was almost certainly a vagrant as I did not have a work permit for the United States. It took two hours of persuasion and the intervention of senior Rotary officials before they reluctantly agreed to allow me back into the United States.

Prior to this experience I had intended to visit Canada during my time at Harvard but I decided against taking this risk in case I was not allowed back into the United States.

At the end of my Harvard year I boarded a Greyhound bus and with a $99 dollar ticket had three months unlimited travel throughout the United States. I visited a number of friends and ended up at Pendleton, Oregon, home of the rodeo where I stayed at the home of a local vet as a guest of the Pendleton Rotary Club. It was quite an experience. I was treated like a celebrity and an aristocratic one at that.

The local radio station interviewed me and I addressed the Rotary Club. I naturally dressed up for the occasion and turned up in a smart suit, white shirt and tie, only to discover that I was the only one wearing either a suit or a tie. I obviously had impressed the chairman who introduced me with the words, "Gentlemen, we are privileged to have as our speaker a genuine young British aristocrat." It was the first and last time I was ever introduced as an aristocrat.

From Pendleton to California, then three days and three nights non-stop to New York and home. I had accepted an offer to be an assistant lecturer in Political Economy at St Andrews. It was time to take life and politics a little more seriously.

eighteenth green at St Andrews Old Course.

Staff at St Andrews had a tremendous lifestyle in those days particularly if you were also a warden, and I eventually became warden of the John Burnet Hall. This position gave me a free flat overlooking St Andrews seventeenth Road Hole. A bachelor, with no mortgage, I ran a small car and one of the perks of the job was that you could enjoy a bottle of wine from the university's fine wine cellars at official functions at no charge, as long as you did not abuse the privilege. I was also a member of the New Club.

The warden's job was to ensure the smooth running of their hall including discipline among the students. I didn't have any problems with my students who were all male. I met their representatives at the start of each session and explained that as an economist I was a follower of Adam Smith, who as they would know was a believer in *laissez faire*. I pointed out that they should know the rules of the hall and I knew the rules. But that as long as they did not bother me I would not bother them.

Rules such as no female students in male students rooms had to be obeyed, and I would prefer not to be placed in an embarrassing position. Most students were discreet and I rarely had any problems.

I was still a Liberal when I returned to St Andrews and was very active for the Liberals during the 1966 General Election when I supported Derek Barrie, who was the Liberal candidate in North East Fife against Sir John Gilmour who held the seat for the Conservatives. Derek and I had been to school together and I ran around the constituency putting up posters and, when the opportunity arose, taking down those belonging to our opponents.

The latter activity got me into some hot water when I spotted a huge Conservative poster attached to a tree in the middle of the countryside. I leapt out of my VW and with the help of my companion began taking the poster down. I was in the middle of this process when a large shooting brake drew up and a rather majestic lady got out and asked, "What are you doing my young man?" I replied that I thought it was disgraceful to spoil the environment by putting such posters on trees, the reply to which was, "It is MY tree, now put it back up." She watched as we put the poster back and then drove off without another word.

After the 1966 General Election in which Labour retained control, I decided that the Conservative Party reflected my political views better than the Liberals. I was influenced by people such as Madsen Pirie and Douglas Mason who were Tories, and I eventually came to the conclusion that the Conservatives represented my train of thought. One of the reasons for my change was that it was clear that there were only two parties who had a chance of forming a Government and if you were serious about politics you had to choose which you wanted to belong to.

I joined the St Andrews branch of the Conservative Association early in 1968, and I was very quickly on the candidates' list for parliamentary seats. There was a lot of activity among Conservative students at that time led by Madsen Pirie, and there was a belief that we should not merely be idealists. We believed in the free market, and believed that we should do something about it, rather than just talk.

The catalyst for action was the Reform Group. Madsen Pirie was President of this group while Douglas Mason was secretary. At that time Madsen was studying philosophy and history and Douglas was an honours graduate in geology. The group took up controversial issues and soon after I joined the Party I was given the job of revising and re-editing a pamphlet which Madsen and Douglas had written in August 1966 about commercial radio entitled *Make it Legal*.

The Labour Government had obviously not paid any attention to what Madsen and Douglas had written for in August 1967 they introduced the Marine Offences Act which made it illegal for British citizens to provide programme material for offshore radio stations or to assist them in any way.

This forced pirate stations such as Radio Caroline off the air but the Reform Group believed strongly in competition and I argued strongly for commercial radio to be legalised. In today's climate this may not seem very radical when few people in my home area don't listen to Radio Clyde 1 or 2, and we have stations such as Scot FM and Classic all fighting for listeners along with BBC's Radio Scotland.

It was very different in the late sixties. Disc jockeys Johnny Walker and Robbie Dale could not return to Britain without risking prosecution. Radio Caroline's headquarters were in Amsterdam in Holland.

Opponents of removing the BBC's monopoly of the airwaves argued that commercial radio would flood the airwaves with pop music and lead to a lowering of standards. In my pamphlet *Freedom in Exile* I argued against this pointing to the experience of Australia and the United States. I wrote:

> The view that monopoly is needed to cater for minority tastes does not really hold, either. The experience of America is that minority tastes will be catered for by private enterprise because although audiences will be smaller, there will be some advertisers who wish to reach this select market.

> Those who argue that programmes of a high cultural level will not be supported by advertising because of the consequential small audience should ask themselves how such stations survive in America, where it is possible to listen to non-stop classical music or current affairs stations.

Events since I wrote these words have proved me correct. We have a commercial station devoted purely to classical music and another to non-stop talk.

In the pamphlet I listed a number of advantages of private enterprise commercial radio. I list them here and allow the reader to judge whether or not my views have been proved correct.

> The need for an audience ensures that concessions are made to public demand and that listeners receive a large proportion of programmes they wish to hear.

> The presence of a larger number of stations gives the listener a much wider choice of programmes.

> Where there are many stations, there are many employers of

writers, musicians and actors and freedom of employment is preserved. A single employer can impose restricting conditions too readily and pay scales need not be competitive.

The competition keeps advertising rates at a keen level and the advertising probably stimulates consumer demand in the same way as Independent Television did.

There are opportunities too, to make more inroads into the vast European consumer market. Some of the pirates were making experiments with foreign language broadcasts, and even their English language broadcasts had continental audience figures running into millions. Radio Caroline receives letters from all over Europe. This audience offers an exciting prospect to British manufacturers and a possible boost to exports.

Programmes of local interest are made available because the audience is more localised.

The multiplicity of channels ensures wider service for minority interests – financed by specialised advertising.

The dangers inherent in the monopoly system are removed. Where there is competition, it is impossible for a small group of like-minded men to put out a one-sided version of current events.

A commercial radio network does not involve additional strain on the pockets of listeners. (There is, in fact, a quite good case to be made out of withdrawing public money from the BBC and abolishing licence fees for both radio and television. The BBC could finance its programmes much more easily from advertisements, and watching or listening to commercials seems a small price to pay for an otherwise free multi-channel radio and television network.)

I ended the pamphlet by drawing attention to the fact that competition supported more choice in television and radio, and finally finished with this call to the pirate radio stations on our high seas:

Until such a government is returned we can only hope that such

champions of freedom as Johnny Walker and Robbie Dale
maintain their lonely vigil on the high seas, accepting their
banishment from our shores as the price of providing pleasure
to millions.

In March 1971 the Conservative Government announced plans for
sixty commercial stations spread throughout the United Kingdom
and in October 1973 the London Broadcasting Company became
the first ever legal competitor to BBC Radio, providing news and
current affairs programmes.

The academic life at St Andrews was a Lotus Land existence
but I knew that it could not last forever. The powers-that-be asked
all lecturers to fill in forms showing what hours we worked. I filled
mine in 'completely honestly' and it proved that I worked ninety
hours a week – after all as a lecturer in Political Economy even
reading the papers could be construed as part of my duties, and if
I had a coffee with some students and discussed how they were
doing then that was also work.

In my off duty hours I played golf but I also spent a great deal
of time in Dundee as I was the prospective Conservative candidate
for Dundee East.

I had been accepted on the candidate's list after an interview
with Sir John Gilmour. In those days becoming a candidate was
much less scientific. It involved obtaining a couple of referees and
going through an interview process. Nowadays a dangerous
radical like myself would not get through the process.

Sir John asked me questions such as why I had switched
political parties and asked if I would be prepared to do a bit of the
hard grind. He also asked if I would be willing to stand in for him
at meetings in the constituency and I readily agreed.

When I became the prospective candidate for Dundee I was
determined to have a real go at improving the Conservative vote
but I did not really expect to win the seat and I still had to assume
that I would earn my living in ways other than as a Member of
Parliament.

Life, as I have said at St Andrews was very pleasant but I

knew that it could not continue forever. Firstly it had already occurred to me that I might want to marry at some point in the future and that would alter my lifestyle dramatically as at that time you could not be married and live in the apartments supplied to wardens.

I also knew that I was never going to be a brilliant economist. The subject was becoming very mathematical and that was not my forte. I was in my late twenties and I realised that I had to move or I would end up perhaps staying at the university forever.

My speciality at university was European Regional Policy and one day my sister Kathleen rang to tell me that there had been an advert in the *Daily Telegraph* from the CBI looking for someone to work in their regional development department. I didn't have any contacts or influence in the CBI but I was given the job and moved to London in January 1971.

The move meant a drop in real income but I was lucky as far as housing was concerned. A friend of mine, Eddie George knew Colin Smith of the *Daily Express* who lived in co-ownership flats in Beckenham, South London. Through Colin I learned that there was a flat available and I managed to obtain it.

Shortly after I arrived in London I met Susie at a party organised by James Davie my senior man at St Andrews who was now living in the Barbican in London. Susie and I knew each other from our university days and we started to go out together. We married in July 1973 in the Crown Court, Church of Scotland in Covent Garden. It is one of only two Church of Scotland's in London and dates back to when James V1 of Scotland became James 1 of England.

## Chapter 3

# RAISING EYEBROWS

I had enjoyed my time at St Andrews both as a student and as a lecturer but if I am honest the highlights of my time spent there revolve around the University of St Andrews Conservative Association. Led by people such as Madsen Pirie and Douglas Mason, the Association proved to be highly effective not only in promoting radical ideas within the Conservative Party but also as a political machine.

Yet, at the same time, it was done with typical student humour. Politics were fun and there is no doubt we caused a few eyebrows to be raised in the Party's Central Office. But no one could deny that we were effective.

We were free marketeers and were seen as a terribly radical

grouping. The Party hierarchy treated us as young people who had to be humoured but we never saw ourselves as being anti-party. In fact, we took the political fight into Labour's heartlands and proved that in unpromising circumstances there was no such thing as a no-go area for Conservatives.

My personal involvement in politics at St Andrews peaked shortly before I left to pursue a career with the CBI in London. I had been chosen as the Conservative Party's parliamentary candidate for Dundee East and fought the seat in the June, 1970 General Election.

George Thomson had held the seat for Labour since winning it in a byelection in 1951. In the 1966 General Election George Thomson had held on the seat beating the Conservative candidate, ex St Andrean, John Marshall by 5,700 votes in a straight fight.

Our Association had been active in the seat and the previous year the Conservative candidate had achieved a good second place in the Hilltown local council elections.

When the General Election arrived we poured students into the constituency. George Thomson was in Labour's Cabinet and was the Government's Mr Europe.

My own view at that time was that we should not go into the European Community. I preferred a loose free trade area which included not only Europe but also North America. The Conservative Party however was in overall favour of entering the Common Market. But this did not prevent us from touring the constituency in a loudspeaker van loaned to us by the Central Office informing the voters that, 'A vote for Stewart is a vote against the Common Market.'

We took this stance partly because of my own personal views, and partly because of George Thomson's position as the Labour Government's man in Europe. I should say at this point that, although I was against going in, I voted Yes in the 1975 Referendum, because by this time we had been members of the Common Market for three years.

I am now in favour of the European Union but I am wholly against the concept of a federal European Super State. I would describe myself as a moderate Euro-sceptic, but I have never voted against the Government on the question. I favour the idea floated by Malcolm Rifkind for some kind of North Atlantic free trade area, a concept I have believed in since my Dundee East days.

In 1970 I could see the humorous side of our anti-Europe campaign although the late Jock Bruce-Gardyne who was defending South Angus was taken aback by our campaign. He complained, with every justification I must say, to Central Office.

However my campaign workers were mainly students, many of whom were not even Tories. They were enjoying the fun of the campaign, and displayed a great deal of student enthusiasm for the cause.

Shortly after the election I wrote the following in *Progressus*, the magazine produced by the Conservative Reform Group at St Andrews:

> Labour's campaign was not much in evidence, perhaps due to the efforts of the worthy native we had met a few days before, going round the constituency with a van and ladder systematically appropriating Thomson posters.

> That was real grass roots support! Labour complaints about midnight vandals removing posters were met with a poker-faced dissertation on Tory law and order policies.

During the campaign I challenged George Thomson, now Lord Thomson of Monefeith, to a public debate, but he was not daft, and quietly told me to get lost.

During the campaign I told everyone that we could beat George. Central Office smiled benignly as we made these claims and nodded their heads. Although when they saw the ballot papers piling up at the count many thought we really could win.

I realised by this time that the swing away from Labour was not big enough. George Thomson was a good MP and was rightfully very popular, and I knew I was not going to take the seat. In the end Labour held on to the seat, although with a much reduced majority of 2,792, the smallest Labour had ever had in this seat. The swing against Labour had been 3.8 per cent which was well above the regional average and twice that in Dundee West.

Our campaign in Dundee East was the culmination of a deliberate policy by the University Conservative Association – and their friends – to go out and campaign in seats where Conservatives had traditionally not done very well.

With some justification we rated ourselves close to Teddy Taylor's election machine in Glasgow Cathcart. Our reputation as the 'St Andrews machine' had begun in October, 1967 when we won, at our second attempt the Glenrothes New Town ward of Rimbleton to gain a seat on Fife County Council.

The Conservative Party at this time was only starting to stand under the Party banner in local council elections. Previously Conservatives had stood as Progressives or as Independents in local elections, or often not at all in Fife.

The Party was standing in only one of the five Glenrothes seats but we persuaded the West Fife Conservative Association to allow Douglas Mason to fight a second Glenrothes seat – Rimbleton. To say the least our prospects were not very hopeful. In the previous 1964 election Labour had a 700 majority over the Communists! On this occasion it was a three way fight between ourselves, Labour and SNP.

To find out what voters were thinking we set up Scottish Statistical Surveys and under the aegis of this organisation, 22 students canvassed the thoughts of almost 4,000 electors.

The results we received were not encouraging: 37% were doubtful; 27% socialist; 21% SNP and only 16% definite Tory voters.

But I thought the figures were not as bad as they first looked. This was a local election and the overall turnout would be low. The key to success was to get our own vote out.

During our campaign, we therefore ignored committed Labour and SNP supporters and concentrated solely on Conservative and possible Conservative supporters. Typically, as our workers were mainly students we were not hidebound by tradition.

One example of this was that we printed our election material in fluorescent red and black instead of the usual blue. This had the result of ensuring that our material stood out. One drawback we later discovered was that douce local Conservative supporters thought they were so gaudy that they refused to put them up in their windows. It seems that many people who may have displayed the traditional blue coloured windows refused to display our startling colours.

St Andrews students we may have been but we were not averse to using every political trick in the book. We produced a hand-out associating the Labour candidate with a recent rent rise. We delayed distributing this particular piece of material until the eve of poll so that Labour would not have time to reply and the leaflet was distributed to all doubtful voters.

Our election day organisation used the NCR (no carbon required) system. The names and addresses of all Conservatives were typed on these pads in street order. Tellers at the gates leading to the polling stations asked all voters their names and addresses and when the lists were brought to our committee rooms we could score off the names of our supporters who had voted. Accepted practice now, but in those days almost unheard of.

We did not win the seat at our first attempt. We came second to the SNP who had gained 755 votes to our 614 and Labour came in third with 432 votes.

However we got a second chance at the seat when the victorious SNP candidate resigned. Our performance during the first election had considerably increased our credibility in the seat.

I was the agent in the byelection which took place during October 1967. The work we had put in during the first campaign meant that we knew where the Tory voters were and we concentrated all our efforts on them. We ran an apparently low-key campaign. Indeed our opponents wrote us off because they believed we were not campaigning. We put out only one pamphlet.

Disaster then struck our deceptive campaign during the mid afternoon of polling day when my car broke down as did another one. This meant we had student workers in St Andrews and voters in Glenrothes but could not get our workers to Rimbleton. We also had the problem that we needed cars to transport our supporters to the polling booths. I phoned Paddy Finlay in Conservative Central Office where we were really considered as slight nutcases.

I told Paddy, "Get me three cars and I will give you a Tory win." He didn't really believe me but to be fair he found the cars and came along himself.

We won in the last hour of the campaign. The Labour Party stopped their campaign at 7.30 pm when they were ahead but we continued to pull our voters out using extra cars belonging to local supporters who had been working during the day. Douglas Mason won 739 votes, Labour 452, SNP 420 and the Communists 40.

St Andrews students had won the Conservatives their first seat on Fife County Council, their first north of the Forth.

We moved on from our success at Rimbleton to Gorgie-Dalry in Edinburgh which was fifty miles from St Andrews. This did not prevent us from providing the candidate, agent and the total organisation of the campaign.

The Conservative Party had never put up a candidate in this seat, which meant that once again we were breaking new ground. Madsen Pirie was our candidate and Richard Henderson the agent. Once again we engaged the services of our own Scottish Statistical Surveys to carry out a sample of the voters. This exercise showed that only 14 per cent of the electorate said they would vote Tory. And we had the added problem that the local Progressives had decided to also stand in the ward. Indeed, they sent an angry letter to Edward Heath, the Party leader demanding that we withdrew from the contest.

We never heard from Heath so we carried on. We ourselves were concerned that the presence of a Progressive on the ballot paper might split the right wing vote. But once again we used what we now termed as The System of Identifying our Supporters.

We distributed a single sheet pseudo newspaper *The Gorgie Tory* to those whom we believed would vote for us and seven St Andrews students delivered 6,000 election addresses while the 'Golf Place Girls' as we called them addressed 2,000 polling cards and envelopes in the weekend before polling day.

We did not win the seat which was taken by the SNP but we were only narrowly beaten into third place by Labour. We collected more than three times the number of votes cast for the Progressives and we showed that the combined right-wing vote equalled the winning SNP vote. We had proved that given a clear run the Conservative Party could win the seat.

Our peers at Central Office were so impressed that they sent us a letter of congratulations and described our performance as "not only the best result in Edinburgh, but by far the best organisation."

During that period in St Andrews the Conservative Association and in particular the Reform Group were questioning many of society's accepted practices. Among these icons of the time was the acceptance that society should pay for a student's university education.

I floated publicly the idea that student grants should be replaced, at least in part, by student loans. Although this has now come to pass with the Students Loans Bill, in 1971 when I wrote a paper entitled *To Him That Hath Shall Be Given* suggesting the introduction of student loans, it was viewed as way-out radical thinking.

I first considered the question of how we finance students in my academic role. In the university's Political Economy department one of the areas I covered was Welfare Economics. This required me to read the entire spectrum of material published on this subject. Among the papers were those from the Institute of Economic Affairs which supported the free market philosophy.

The Institute's director Ralph Harris had started a debate on the question of student grants vis-a-vis loans. My natural instinct is towards nineteenth century liberalism and I became convinced that the State was doing many things which were counter productive, and that there were too many controls. I became convinced that students grants were regressive and that huge amounts of taxpayers' money were going to people who were privileged anyway.

The issue was debated by students within the department and although not all students agreed with my views, the debate was intellectually exciting. I had to be careful when marking essays to ensure that I marked fairly those people who disagreed with me. If anything I think I probably over-compensated to ensure fairness.

Eventually the academic debate entered into the political arena and shortly before I left the university, I wrote the *To Him That Hath Shall Be Given* essay which the Conservative Association published along with other essays on university issues in 1971.

I wrote in the introduction:

> For long, the loans versus grants arguments has seemed merely an intellectual exercise. Now, however, with a significant shift in public opinion and the advent of a government apparently prepared to stand up against powerful pressure groups the debate takes on a new urgency.
>
> This is not to deny that a change to loans would meet with vehement, vocal and possibly violent opposition. The abolition of privilege is never painless.

I used as an example to argue my case that of two fictitious brothers.

> Brother Algernon invests in his future by going to university. Brother Joe invests in his future by setting up a fish and chip shop. He receives no state assistance – on the contrary he is heavily taxed from the start. His taxes in effect, help to pay for Brother Algernon's investment.
>
> If unsuccessful, Algernon has no debts while Joe faces bankruptcy. If successful, both will earn higher incomes than they otherwise would have. Why should the investment of the one be provided free?

I argued that most of the tax revenue was gathered from the ordinary man and women in the street while three out of four students came from middle and upper class homes.

To answer the argument that the government gets back the money they give in student grants in the shape of income tax, I stated:

> Why not give business men free factories, trainee pop singers free electric guitars or aspiring ice cream vendors free vans and musical chimes? All these free investments would doubtless assist the worthy citizens involved to earn higher incomes and so pay more tax than they otherwise would.

On the question of society gaining benefit from Brother Algernon going to university I then wrote:

> Certainly Brother Algernon may make important contributions to the progress of ideas, his skills may be the key to a significant scientific breakthrough, his conversation may elevate his less privileged friends. (On the other hand he may now bore them rigid, thus creating significant diseconomies!)

> But what of Brother Joe? Does his income measure the total gain to the social weal from his activities? By no means. His cheap, nourishing meals may keep alive many old folks with consequent benefits to their friends and relations. If Joe is situated near a pub, the sobering effects of his fish suppers may significantly reduce death on the roads, and so on.

The essay concluded:

> In the short term at least, a loans scheme would be administered and financed by government, with loans varying by course, not by individual to avoid discrimination. But there is every reason to hope that private loan capital would increasingly enter the market.

It took a long time for the issue to come before Parliament, but when it did I supported it strongly. My views on this issue have not changed although I would illustrate them differently now. My original paper addressed a student readership who enjoyed a more off-beat approach to serious subjects, an approach I do not disagree with as too often we politicians bore our audiences with long tedious speeches.

I strongly support the principle of student loans because although there is a general benefit to society from higher education there is also a benefit to the individual. Yes, there should be a contribution from the taxpayer, but there should also be a contribution from the student.

During the Student Loans Bill's progress through Parliament I volunteered to serve on the committee which looked at it line by line and I addressed the House of Commons on the subject when the Bill was receiving its second reading.

Prior to the Bill being introduced I had spoken in favour of such a measure to Ministers and also to Mrs Eleanor Laing who was John McGregor's special advisor on education.

My views on the existing student loans scheme is that although in general it is working, there are several changes that should be made to it. I would increase the amount a student could borrow quite sharply and would check how the present method of repayments is working based on experience. I supported the second Bill in 1995 to allow the banks to participate in the scheme.

## CHAPTER 4

# BRITISH INDUSTRY

My first day in my new job in 1971 at the Confederation of British Industry was January 1, not the most auspicious of days for a Scot to start a new job.

I had attended a Hogmanay party the previous evening but did not touch a drop of alcohol as I was determined to have a clear head, and arrive on time on my first day. My strategy worked. I did arrive prompt at 9am only to discover that I was the only one in the office – everyone else wandered in around 10 o'clock!

Campbell Adamson was the Director of the CBI at the time and my position was a middle management one as a head of a department reporting directly to one of the deputy directors. My responsibility was to develop the CBI's regional development policy and also examine the relationship between the State and Industry.

The CBI is made up of firms of varied sizes including the nationalised industries. British industry was not very efficient during this period. We were losing market share quite considerably to our competitors in Japan, Europe and North America. There were a number of problems which industry in general had not faced up to. Productivity levels were low and the trade unions were in a powerful position while management was not very self confident. Our investment record was also poor compared to other countries such as Japan.

In 1973 I was appointed deputy director of economic department at the CBI, which had become a powerful position around that particular period because the organisation had decided for the first time to issue an annual policy statement.

I was placed in charge of co-ordinating the operation by bringing the various strands from the different departments together, then writing the document.

The CBI took the decision to publish such a statement very seriously and, as the official responsible, I reported to the late Lord Watkinson who was chairman of Cadbury Schweppes, and chairman of the CBI committee responsible for the report.

The objective was for the CBI to stop merely reacting to what everyone else was saying and to put our own point of view forward, and to make a case for responsible capitalism.

Although I co-ordinated the document it was subject of course to policy makers such as Lord Watkinson whose experience of government was invaluable. He had a brilliant ability to concentrate on essentials.

My arrival at the CBI had coincided with a great debate on what road capitalism was going down. Ted Heath, as Prime Minister, had in May 1973 made his statement about the activities of Lonrho. He described the group's activities as "the unacceptable face of capitalism." The CBI were worried that in the public mind the controversy surrounding Lonrho would destroy the case for free enterprise.

The situation was treated very seriously but I can recall one incident when it brought a touch of humour to the proceedings. It was during a CBI Council meeting when the President asked the gathering, "What is the pleasant and acceptable face of capitalism?" At this point Campbell Adamson rose to his feet to widespread hilarity.

The debate around State intervention sharpened when Harold Wilson won the March 1974 General Election and Tony Benn became Industry Minister.

It will not surprise anyone if I place on record the fact that I totally disagreed with Benn's policy of State controls and intervention but I have to say that when I first saw him in action he was absolutely brilliant. He had been invited to address the CBI in Wales. Wrongly in my view there was a discussion among some members as to whether or not they should attend. But this was ludicrous. Industrialists cannot ignore whoever is the Secretary of State for Industry. I was asked to attend the meeting as the Head Office specialist on state intervention.

Benn knew that he would be facing a hostile audience, but he started by explaining how he came from a family business background. He said he appreciated that those present did not agree with him, but that he had great sympathy for those small firms who suffered when large firms exercised their power unreasonably by not paying their bills on time. It was a clever way of bringing a hostile audience round to his side. Benn throughout spoke in his usual quiet manner and I will never forget that occasion as he handled his audience so well.

At the height of the Bennery period Campbell Adamson summoned me to his office. He told me that he had received a call from the *Daily Express* asking him to write an article explaining why the CBI was against Tony Benn's proposals.

As usual the paper wanted the article almost immediately. The deadline was 1pm and it was already mid morning. I told Campbell it was impossible, but he managed to persuade me to write the draft by explaining that although the article would be in his name he would pass the £100 fee on to me. This monetary offer overcame my misgivings and by noon I had a draft article on his desk.

After he had made one or two changes it was sent off to the *Express*. I duly received the £100 and Susie and I bought a freezer with the money. It was the first luxury article we had bought in our marriage.

My work at the CBI brought me into contact with a number of politicians at that time and among those I met then were Michael Heseltine, who was the Shadow Secretary for Industry when Tony Benn was Secretary of State. And earlier, during the period when the Conservatives were in power, I had contact with Peter Walker during his time as Secretary of State for Trade and Industry.

Peter Walker was a very astute politician. Some members of the CBI were concerned about the quality and price of steel they were receiving from British Steel and a meeting was arranged with Peter Walker to raise their concerns. Instead of taking the burden on the Government, Peter Walker immediately suggested that a working group should be set up on which both British Steel and their customers would sit on. I chaired most of the working meetings and we did resolve the problem by the two sides sitting down together.

Despite my responsibilities at the CBI I still managed to keep up my interest in politics, and remained on the Conservative Party's candidates' list.

I was interviewed for a number of Scottish seats and reached the shortlist for three, Edinburgh North, Bute and North Ayrshire, Kelvingrove as well as the longlist for East Fife.

I was not selected for any of these seats, mainly I believe, because I was living in England, and the constituency parties were worried about my ability to campaign in the constituency prior to the main election campaign due to the travel involved. This was totally understandable.

However I did represent the Conservative Party as a local councillor while I was in London, and I had to defeat John Major for the privilege.

After we were married in 1973 Susie and I bought a small

terraced house in Shortlands, near Bromley South Station in the Beckenham constituency. I was the Treasurer of the Beckenham Conservative Association.

The local councillor became an alderman and this created a byelection for his seat on the London Borough of Bromley Council. John Major was among those who put himself forward for the seat, but I won the nomination 5-4 to become the candidate, mainly I believe because I lived in the ward.

When the byelection was held in 1975 it was a three way fight between ourselves, Labour and Liberals, but it was a Tory seat and we received 88 per cent of the vote.

Being a councillor was hard work. Committee meetings were held at 7.30 pm in the evenings which meant councillors work a full day before going on to the meeting. And for all councillors the volume and complexity of paper work was considerable.

But my workload as a councillor lasted less than two years as Hamish Grant, secretary of the CBI in Scotland was retiring in 1976, and I decided to apply for the position.

I had always seen myself as being Scottish, although not in a nationalistic sense, and had always intended to return home to Scotland when a suitable opportunity arose. Within the CBI in Scotland the position of secretary was the only Scottish job equivalent to the position I held in London.

John Methven had succeeded Campbell Adamson as Director of the CBI by this time, and I had developed a good working relationship with him. He did not want me to apply for the Scottish position. I had been heavily involved in ensuring that the CBI's viewpoint on a number of issues had been publicly aired and the organisation was becoming more proactive. He told me that he preferred that I stayed in London and suggested I withdraw my application. I refused, although I thanked him for his comments.

There was no extra money involved as the deputy director position I held in London was considered to be on the same level as the Scottish position.

Two days later he called me into his office and told me, " I am not sure you are doing the right thing but you have got the job." John Methven was a talented person and a first class successor to Campbell Adamson as CBI Director General but he died not long after I returned to Scotland. He never stopped working. He died in hospital and was still reading briefing papers despite being ill.

Susie and I moved back to Scotland in November 1976. We had bought a grey sandstone semi-detached house in Rowan Road, Dumbreck on the south side of Glasgow near Ibrox without my even seeing it. My mother and father helped in our house hunting and they had spotted this particular house and suggested that it was the type we were looking for. Susie flew up to Glasgow on the Saturday on her own to have a look at it as we could not afford for both of us to fly up and down to Scotland looking for houses.

The seller wanted to complete the deal quickly but there was only one slight problem. Both my mother and Susie had seen the house, and both described it to me in great detail but they couldn't agree on basic details such as whether or not it had a driveway.

I phoned Ronnie Dundas, the City Editor of *The Herald* whom I had known since my St Andrews University days and asked for his views on the locality. We bought the house on the Monday and I never regretted the decision.

It was a lovely family house in a very convenient location and we had great neighbours. The late Jimmy McGrory, manager of Celtic and his wife Barbara were nextdoor. They were wonderful people. Scot Symon the former Rangers manager lived behind us.

At the CBI in Scotland from 1976–79 there were a number of major issues to be dealt with including our views on the Bullock Committee which proposed requiring companies to set up workers' councils, and of course the Labour Government's proposal for constitutional change.

Both proposals were strongly opposed. Companies wanted good relations with their own employees – that is in their own interests. But they did not wish to be forced by the state into a particular format. Business remained profoundly sceptical about constitutional change which could be costly and result in continuing uncertainty.

During my period in charge of the CBI in Scotland I worked with several excellent chairmen and leaders including Alan Devereux , Douglas Hardie, David (now Lord) Nickson, Jim (now Lord) Goold and Norman (now Lord) Macfarlane of Bearsden.

The job obviously brought me into contact with Scottish Office Ministers. Since Labour was in power at the time, I mostly dealt with the late Gregor MacKenzie who had responsibility for industry. It was hard to criticise Gregor who took his job very seriously and did it very well. He became a good friend and he was not a man of the left.

From time to time we also had occasion to meet Bruce Millan who was Secretary of State for Scotland and whom CBI members quite rightly respected for his work and his command of detail.

At this stage I was still on the Conservative Party's candidates' list but due to pressure of work commitments I had spoken to Graham McMillan at the Party's Edinburgh head-quarters to ask for my name to be frozen. This meant that my political career was really in limbo. I was still on the list but I was under no obligation to apply for every vacant seat which arose.

This was the position in 1978 when I heard that Betty Harvie Anderson was not proposing to stand again in the East Renfrew-shire seat. At that time everyone expected Jim Callaghan, who was the Labour Prime Minister at the time, to call a General Election in the autumn.

Several Glasgow businessmen approached me to enquire whether or not I was putting my name forward. They normally started the conversation by saying that they had heard that I had put my hat in the ring. When I had to deny this, the conversation would then lead on to what support I could expect if I did become a candidate. The feeling emerged that I would be a credible and serious contender.

Susie and I talked it over. It was a big decision. I had a good job with a good salary and a position in public life. It was a terrible dilemma. We finally decided that I should go for the nomination as I knew that if I had not put my name forward I would have spent the rest of my life asking myself why I hadn't taken the risk.

When it became known that I was going to be a candidate John Methven expressed his disappointment and told me that I had a good future with the CBI.

I reminded John that the CBI had just brought out a booklet saying that companies should encourage their employees to stand for election, and were advocating that one way they could do this was to help with pensions, and to keep a person's job open for seven years to reduce the risk of someone losing their seat, having given up a secure career. John got the message and wished me well.

I reached the shortlist for the seat along with three other candidates, one of whom was Reg Prentice the former Labour Minister. The interviews were to be held in the RSAC premises in Blythswood Square, Glasgow.

The constituency did not want to have newspapers and television doorstepping the meeting but someone had leaked the fact that Reg Prentice was on the shortlist and where the meeting was being held.

To avoid the waiting press we were sneaked into the building via the adjoining McTaggart and Mickel premises which gave us access to the RSAC cellars! It was all rather bizarre and as it turned out a waste of time, for when we eventually reached the floor on which the meeting was being held, we were confronted by a journalist who asked Reg Prentice what he thought his chances were.

Everyone had forgotten that journalists are entitled to be members of the RSAC and this newspaper representative had used his club membership to walk through the front door and up to the meeting room.

The fact that a former Labour Minister was standing had meant there was huge press interest in who gained the nomination. I had phoned Douglas Mason to say that I thought I had a good chance but that I hoped that no paper such as the *Sunday Express* would carry any stories indicating this. Ordinary members resent any suggestion that they are being told how to vote by the press. I couldn't believe my eyes when I opened my *Scottish Sunday Express* on the week-end before the shortlist interviews to see a story saying that I would beat Reg Prentice for the seat.

All the candidates were accompanied by their spouses but we were told that spouses would not be asked any questions. I felt the meeting was going quite well. I had been asked a question about Prices and Incomes policy, a subject on which I was well versed, and I had denounced the idea that any Government should try and interfere with the market in this way as the whole concept was unworkable. My reply received polite applause from the sixty or so people present.

Then out of the blue someone rose and asked Susie if she would speak and support me if I became MP for the constituency. Susie was taken by surprise as she was not expecting to answer any questions but she rose and said that she would support me absolutely but that she never made public speeches. This reply seemed to be very popular. Many constituency councillors and activists rightly do not want an MP's wife to interfere. Ever since, Susie has been a quiet but tremendous support in the constituency.

I won the nomination and later discovered that one of the reasons for my victory was that the constituency party had a solid unionist majority who were against devolution, and of course my opposition to this policy was well known.

Betty Harvie Anderson's role in the selection procedure was that she had the power within the constituency to effectively veto a candidate but she did not of course have the power to deliver the nomination for any single candidate. That was entirely a matter for individual members of the executive in a secret ballot.

Having won the nomination and become the prospective Conservative Candidate for East Renfrewshire as the constituency was known then, I immediately began to campaign. The entire selection process had been done as quickly as possible as we expected a General Election to be called almost immediately. I can remember watching the famous Callaghan appearance on television when he announced that he was NOT calling an election in October 1978. I was pouring over maps of the constituency at the time, and I just fell back in my seat. I couldn't believe it.

He should have called an election. It would have been a tough battle and the result would have been desperately close but I believe Labour would have fared better than they did the following year after the Winter of Discontent.

My campaign during the General Election was purely on the party ticket. However being a new candidate has its advantages. The constitutency then as now was extremely fortunate in its leading office bearers. It is easy to underestimate how much commitment lies behind the purely voluntary and often tremendous efforts of party volunteers.

l had gained some experience of campaigning in the constituency prior to the General Election of 1979 because of a local council byelection in the Kirkhill ward of Newton Mearns when we had easily beaten the SNP candidate by around nine to one.

It had been a new experience for me because until then all my electioneering in Scotland had been in Labour strongholds. At the General Election we pushed the majority up very sharply in East Renfrewshire and won by 12,176 votes.

It was back to London again. Susie and I didn't have any family at that point. We obviously kept our family home in Dumbreck and I rented a small flat in Tower Hill. It was on the top floor of a vicarage which George Thompson, the SNP Member of Parliament, had previously occupied.

I only stayed in this flat for a short while before the Duchy of Cornwall, whom I had approached earlier, contacted me to say they had a flat available overlooking Kennington Oval cricket ground. It was a small flat with a bedroom, sitting room, study, kitchen and bathroom. This is still my London home, and I can watch the cricket matches by standing on a chair on the balcony. I'm sure the neighbours describe me as that "bloody mean Scot."

## CHAPTER 5

# JOINING THE GOVERNMENT

My first position of responsibility in Government was as always on the first step of the ladder. In April 1981 I became Parliamentary Private Secretary to Hamish Gray, Minister of State at the Department of Energy. This is an unpaid position and is looked upon as the point of entry for possible Ministerial office.

I remained in this junior position in the Department of Energy for almost six months. Above me in the department were John Moore and Norman Lamont who were both Under Secretaries to David Howell.

Then in September 1981 I became an Under Secretary of State at the Scottish Office with responsibility for Health and Social Work.

I was offered the position by Margaret Thatcher after receiving a phone call at my desk from a member of her staff who asked, "Is that Allan Stewart, member for Renfrew?" I replied, slightly annoyed, "Allan Stewart, member for East Renfrewshire!" Then Margaret came on the phone. She had overheard this and thought it quite funny.

One of my most vivid memories of this period was my own real life version of the TV series *Yes Minister*. It was a very good programme, and I recall watching one particular episode which was built round a new hospital which had everything but patients. The following morning I had a meeting with senior civil servants and asked if they had seen the programme the previous evening. Back came the chorus, "Yes, Minister." I chuckled, "We don't have any hospitals like that, do we?" There was a hush and a shuffling of feet and one of the civil servants present looking rather embarrassed replied, "Well, there is that kind of problem. . . ."

It then emerged that in Greenock we had the situation where a new hospital had been built, but there was a wing lying empty. The comedy programme had in fact highlighted a real problem faced by those running the health service at that time. This was that major capital programmes can run for several years and that sometimes the timing of completion is practically impossible to forecast.

This meant that the forecasts for running costs could become out of phase with the capital costs. This is what had happened at Greenock. Having been made aware of the Greenock situation I told the civil servants that they had better resolve the situation, and they did.

An Under Secretary of State at the Scottish Office is ultimately responsible for a large department with spending budgets of hundreds of millions of pounds. Back-up consists of a private office at St Andrews House in Edinburgh where you have a staff consisting of a private secretary with an assistant and a clerk.

Scottish Office Ministers such as Michael Forsyth and Malcolm Rifkind who became Ministers at Whitehall were, I know, immediately struck by how much bigger the staffs of Whitehall Ministers are.

George Younger was Scottish Secretary of State when I joined the team and he believed in delegating responsibility which allowed his Ministers a great deal of freedom. There was a meeting under George Younger every Wednesday morning at Dover House in London. At this meeting Ministers and senior civil servants raised issues which required a collective discussion.

There were also individual meetings with the Secretary of State to discuss matters which your department felt should be brought to the attention of the Scottish Secretary or indeed matters which you personally wished to discuss with the Secretary of State.

In 1982 after Malcolm Rifkind moved to the Foreign Office I was made Under Secretary of State at the Scottish Office with responsibilities for Home Affairs and the Environment. It was a bigger job in that it was likely to be more controversial.

I was responsible for the police and local government finance. My new responsbilities included overseeing the running of Scotland's prisons which led me on occasions to visit HM Prison establishments from time to time including the Special Unit at Barlinnie which is now closed.

One of my first duties as the Government Minister responsible for Scottish prisons was to announce £4 million of additional investment which included the building of twenty new single cells at Barlinnie to help relieve overcrowding. I went along to the prison to see current conditions at first hand and visited the Special Unit which until three months before had housed its most famous inmate Jimmy Boyle.

There was the usual media coverage and as the Government had earmarked £100,000 for improving the kitchens, several newspapers carried photographs the next day of me tasting some prison chips.

The point was to try to create a positive image that prisons should be about the future of people as well as their behaviour in the past.

The lack of a person's freedom should be the punishment.

We should not brutalise prisoners during their sentence, and the treatment of prisoners should be civilised. I am a strong supporter of prison industries, not merely because they make money for the system, and therefore save the taxpayer money, but also working while in prison allows inmates to do something constructive, and to learn new skills which they can use when they have completed their sentences.

It is important that we keep the correct balance in prison life as they are in many ways communities although obviously prison officers are in an entirely different position from those they guard. Although the regime must prevent escapes, if it becomes too restrictive that can create problems within prison establishments. Although I am strongly in favour of Michael Howard's move towards minimum sentencing there has to be an incentive within the prison parole system for early release. This may not be a view universally accepted within Tory Party ranks but if there is no incentive given as a reward for good behaviour then people are going to behave badly.

Private prisons now operate in England, and I do not see any reason why we cannot go further down this route. Of course the Government must be careful about who they gave such contracts to but fundamentally there is no reason why more private prisons should not be built and operated in the future.

My new responsibilites also meant that I had to deal with local councils throughout Scotland, many of whom were dominated by Labour, and as you would expect, hostile to Government policies. At times they did their best to frustrate our reforms.

My first major battle with the Labour councils was over the sale of council houses. This is another example of a Tory Government measure which the Labour Party opposed when it was first introduced but which they now agree with.

However in 1983 Labour were still opposed to our legislation and a number of councils were doing their best to prevent their tenants from buying their own homes. I had to reprimand Glasgow and Aberdeen for allowing a backlog to develop in the processing of council house sales.

The Scottish Development Department produced figures which showed that more than 2000 tenants had waited longer than the statutory two months for the council to put a price on their house. I warned seventeen district councils including Dundee and Motherwell that they were dragging their feet and said at the time that tenants were being denied their right to buy their homes within the reasonable time limit laid down in the Tenants Rights Act.

An example of the attempts to prevent council house sales was Glasgow District Council's insistence that tenants who wanted to have their homes modernised had to sign a contract restricting their rights to buy. The reality was that these contracts were unenforceable as a specific clause in the Local Government and Planning (Scotland) Act 1982 stated that no agreement could restrict a tenant's right to buy their house.

I often wonder what those tenants, who were misled and who had obstacles placed in their way when they first tried to buy their council home, think about it all now as they enjoy the benefits of home ownership – particularly now that Labour has been converted to the Conservative way of thinking.

Council house sales is the biggest single social change we have introduced in Scotland. Prior to 1979 Scotland had a lower ratio of owner-occupiers than Eastern European countries or Cuba. The policy has been a tremendous success, but I am disappointed that it has not resulted in former council house tenants voting for the Conservative Party which gave them the right to buy. There is evidence that voters switched their allegiance in England but it may be in Scotland that in part it was the already Tory-inclined tenants who bought their council houses.

More than 200,000 homes have been sold since we introduced the right for sitting tenants to buy their council houses in the Tenants' Rights (Scotland Act) 1980. The legislation also covered Scottish Special Housing Association stock. Our target at the time was to sell 10% of the 894,549 homes involved and I am delighted that we are now well past this figure. This sea change in housing is so important for a free market because it is irreversible. Any future Labour Government may wish to amend the existing legislation but they would not be able to reverse what has already happened. Our right to buy policy is an extension of an individual's choice. It gives those who buy a stake in the free enterprise housing market.

Local authority spending was another issue which led to us being at loggerheads with councils. I went into the lions' den to make the Government's position regarding overspending when I addressed the Convention of Scottish Local Authorities annual conference in Inverness in March 1983. At this meeting I warned the councils present that the Government would consider taking action against councils whose planned expenditure was significantly in excess of Government guidelines.

The Prime Minister called a June General Election but as a Government Minister my responsibilities continued during the Election campaign.

George Younger had asked Lothian, Glasgow, Kirkcaldy, Stirling and Shetland to justify their spending of ratepayers' money and asked them to explain their spending decisions by June 6. The General Election was called for June 9 but I made it clear that the Government still expected to receive their details by the due date.

One of the biggest decisions I took while carrying out my responsibilities was to delay the scheduled rating revaluation. I was very uneasy about the revaluation going ahead and I asked the Civil Servants at St Andrews House what the effects of it were likely to be.

They told me they did not know, but I replied that I believed it would lead to the burden being transferred to the domestic ratepayer. This was because the revaluation of business premises was likely to lead to commercial firms paying less, but the local authorities would still need to raise the same amount of revenue, and would have to turn to the domestic rates to raise the funds.

I told the civil servants to find me a technical reason to delay the revaluation as with a General Election looming I quite frankly did not wish to push ahead with an action which would be electorally unpopular and undermine the credibility of the whole system. There was some criticism of my action in the Commons but I managed to use a great deal of technical jargon and make it sound boring. From that particular late night debate I suspect only Gordon Wilson, the then MP for Dundee East, really understood the intricacies. Most people, like that greatest Scottish Tory of them all, Lord Home of the Hirsel, did not want to tangle with the rating system. The revaluation of course had to go ahead after the General Election but it was left to Michael Ancram to carry it through, and what I feared would happen was proved to be correct. It was not a popular action as my constituency mail bag hugely demonstrated.

The General Election was due to be held on June 9, 1983, and I was opposed by James McGuire, a Strathclyde Regional councillor and former provost of Barrhead who stood for Labour, Jenny Herriot, who worked in the National Health Service who was the SNP candidate and James Pickett, Director of the David Livingstone Institute of Overseas Development at Strathclyde University, who carried the SDP/Alliance banner in the election.

The constituency had changed since I had won the seat in 1979 by 11,500, the Party's largest majority in Scotland. The Boundary Commission had removed Elderslie and Ralston from the constituency which meant that the electorate was 8,000 fewer. The name of the constitency was changed too, from East Renfrewshire to Eastwood.

I fought the election on the Government's record and through our local *Mercury* paper told voters at the time,

> The Government through sturdy, sound economic policies has brought inflation down to 4 per cent – the lowest level for 15 years. That is the basis for economic recovery. Lower taxes and costs give incentives for companies to expand. Tough decisions have been faced squarely to get the economy back on a common-sense course.

As Scottish Office Minister with responsibility for housing I attended a party press conference in Edinburgh where I attacked Labour's attitude towards the sale of council houses and highlighted the fact that a Labour Government would end the right of tenants to buy their council house, and that those who had already bought their houses would be prevented from selling them on the open market. Labour have since abandoned this policy, and accept that our policy in this field was correct.

I attracted 21,072 votes, a majority of 8,595 over my nearest opponent, Jim Pickett of the SDP/Alliance who polled 12,477 votes.

Labour received 9,083 votes while the SNP candidate came last with 2,618 votes.

I do not believe that the Eastwood electorate were impressed by the SNP candidate's past record which included chaining herself to the gates of the closed Talbot factory when the equipment was being auctioned off. She also did not help her campaign when she told the *Scotsman* newspaper, "Of course Allan Stewart is going to win. It is a foregone conclusion." Very good on honesty, a bit low on political subtlety. I never shared these views but I was pleased with the result having received 46.6 per cent of the vote.

Following the Election Alex Fletcher was transferred from the Scottish Office to the Department of Trade and Industry and I was given responsibilty at the Scottish Office for Industry and Education which was a more high profile position than my status as Minister for Home Affairs and the Environment.

My new responsibilities attracted some press comment and John McKinlay in the *Glasgow Herald* drew attention to the fact that my responsibilities would include the Scottish Development Agency and Locate in Scotland.

The article recalled that three years earlier I had been in part responsible along with Ian Lang for drafting a chapter in a Select Committee report which called for the closure of Scotland's job hunting offices abroad so we could fall in with the UK effort.

I did not find it difficult to explain that I fully supported Locate in Scotland, pointing out that the Select Committee had been worried about the duplication of effort abroad and the confusion which arose by the unco-ordinated approach by the SDA, Scottish local authorities and new towns. The Government answered this criticism by introducing a single door approach in the form of Locate in Scotland.

But it was my other responsbility, education which was to cause me the most heartache and trouble during this period when the main teachers union, Educational Institute of Scotland, launched a campaign of industrial action over pay and conditions.

There had been rumblings of discontent among teachers for some time but in October 1984 the EIS leadership demanded an independent review of salaries. The union threatened to sabotage moves towards the new Standard Grade exams which were being introduced as a result of the Munn and Dunning reports.

George Younger, who was Secretary of State at the time, refused the EIS demands and the union announced a campaign to target primary and secondary schools in my consituency and also George's, as well as those in the constituencies of other Scottish Office ministers.

The union was also very clever. It did not impose a heavy financial burden on its members by restricting the strikes to Tuesday, Wednesday and Thursdays of each week when they knew that teachers were in effect paid for a seven day week.

The industrial action began in January 1985, and the only way out of it for the Government was to stump up more money or concede to the EIS demands for a committee of enquiry. I found it very difficult personally because I had an uneasy suspicion that the teachers had a case, but the Treasury would not move a muscle.

The decision to target schools in Ministers' constituencies made life very difficult. Inevitably people were saying why is my child's education being destroyed because you are a Government Minister? But the Government could not possibly give into this type of pressure, otherwise where would it stop?

During the dispute Margaret Thatcher visited Eastwood to meet constituency workers and the EIS picketed Eastwood House where we were meeting.

We offered the teachers a four year deal worth £125 million

in return for changes in their conditions of working but this was refused and the strikes continued. The EIS also threatened to boycott the 1986 examinations but the union recognised that public opinion was moving against them and dropped their tactic of targetting the schools in Ministers' constituencies.

Malcolm Rifkind, took over as Secretary of State when George Younger moved to the Ministry of Defence, but the dispute still dragged on. The Government finally agreed to set up a General Committee of Enquiry into teachers' pay and conditions.

I must say I was delighted it was all over. It had been a very difficult period for me partly because I knew that the teachers had something of a case. I was caught between having to take a strong line against the union's actions while at the same time being extremely concerned about the workload teachers had to carry.

It was not only what the EIS was saying to us, but what individual teachers were telling me when I met them. I was officially in charge of handling the Government's case and it put me through a great deal of mental anguish. I knew that the Government could not concede to the targetting of schools in Government Ministers' constituencies but at the same time children were suffering.

I however could not express my personal views because quite rightly I had to abide by the collective Government view. A Government could not operate without collective responsibility. I resigned my ministerial position in the Scottish Office in September 1986 but I was asked to return after the 1987 General Election. I refused.

Some people suggested that this was because I could not work with Malcolm Rifkind. This was not true. My decision was not a political one. I had no qualms about working with Malcolm but during the teachers' dispute my personal health had suffered because of the heavy commitments. My working day would start at 9am and last right through to 1am the next morning. MPs, like everyone else, have family commitments. Your children are only young once.

There was also the fact that I had had the practical experience of having to take collective responsibility for a policy that adveresly affected my constituency. At the time I decided that I would never be a Government Minister again.

## CHAPTER 6

# POWER FROM THE BACKBENCHES

My return to the back benches in September 1986 gave me the freedom to campaign on issues which as a Government Minister I had been prevented from acting on.

I had barely had time to draw my breath as a backbencher when Ian Imrie, the late air correspondent of the *Glasgow Herald* rang me to enquire what, if anything, I had decided to campaign on? I knew Ian well as he was also the industrial correspondent of the paper, and he had been in regular touch with me when I had Ministerial responsibility for industry at the Scottish Office. I immediately told him that I would be fighting to for an 'open skies' policy which would allow transatlantic flights to use Glasgow or Edinburgh airports instead of being forced to use Prestwick.

Ian was a very experienced journalist and I am sure that he had a good idea what I was going to say when he asked me the question. Although the Government officially supported the free market, it was common knowledge that the official view did not appear to extend to opening up Scotland's airways. Everything had to stop at Prestwick Airport.

George Younger consistently mounted a strong defence of the status quo and he was ably supported by another local Ayrshire MP, Labour's George Foulkes. The business community in Scotland were privately livid over the Government's stance, and Robin Duthie, chairman of the Scottish Development Agency shared my views.

During the period 1979 to 1983 part of Glasgow Airport had been in my constituency when it covered Linwood, Elderslie and a slither of the airport. Even at that time Glasgow Airport was the biggest single employer in the area but it was rapidly losing ground to Manchester which was becoming a major hub airport.

My campaign started off innocuously by asking questions in Parliament. Paul Channon, the Secretary of State for Transport confirmed that the Prestwick monopoly was to remain although in 1988 when he was no longer Transport Secretary he told the Scottish Conservative Annual Conference in Perth that airlines should be able to choose their own routes. He took credit for the fact that Britain had been at the forefront of a seven year battle to deregulate aviation throughout the Common Market. The result he said had been better services at a lower cost.

The debate was not taking place in the House of Commons but through the Scottish media. In mid-1989 the Government decided to carry out a review and I published a booklet *Landing Right* through the Adam Smith Institute to argue against the status quo. The booklet stated bluntly that the Government's decision had won it few friends outside of Ayrshire.

The Scottish CBI, Scotland's Chambers of Commerce, local councils, tourist authorities and major firms were, I said, united with international airlines in deploring the decision which flew in the face of commercial common sense. Prestwick had originally been chosen as Scotland's transatlantic airport because it could provide landing and take-off flight paths over open flat countryside or over the sea and had a relatively fog-free environment.

Technology however had overtaken these reasons. Aircraft design and engine power made shorter and steeper take-offs possible, and aircraft could land by instrument. Scotland was losing out because of the Government's insistence on defending Prestwick.

Despite the huge growth in air travel fewer passengers were using Prestwick than ten years previously. A 1988 survey had revealed that only around a third of Scots flying across the Atlantic travelled via Prestwick and among business travellers the proportion fell to a fifth. Many flew to London to catch flights but an increasing number were travelling to Manchester which was marketing itself abroad as the 'Gateway to Scotland!'

My campaign continued during the review period but only two MPs offered any real support – David Marshall, who had an interest in transport matters, and the late Allen Adams, MP for Paisley North. I prepared briefing papers *The Myths of the Monopolists* which I distributed among those supporting the campaign.

The Government insisted that we could not have transatlantic flights into other Scottish airports without the agreement of the Americans, and that this was the subject of a bilateral agreement. I discovered that this was not the case when Charles H Dudley, the Civil Aviation Attache replied to a letter I had written to him on July 27, 1989.

In his reply of August 21, Charles Dudley said,

> Unfortunately, however Glasgow's present attractiveness as a traffic point for US airlines is diminished by the requirement that non-European flights to/from Scotland use Prestwick airport.
>
> This requirement is not a consequence of the Bermuda 2 agreement, and the UK Government assured the US

Government in 1978 that if Glasgow airport becomes available
for long-haul services, it will become available to both
scheduled and charter services on a non-discriminatory basis."

This was an important revelation. Both Labour and Conservative
governments had hidden behind the existence of the Bermuda 2
agreement claiming that it allowed for only one transatlantic
gateway airport in Scotland, and that a choice had therefore to be
made between Prestwick, Glasgow or Edinburgh. The reality was
that it was the UK Government alone that was standing in the way
of an open sky policy. I made it my business to establish exactly
when in 1978 the Government had made their views known to the
United States Government.

I obtained a copy of a letter from Mr W P Shovelton, at the
Department of Trade in London, dated April 25, 1978 to Mr James
Atwood, deputy assistant secretary for transportation at the US
State Department which stated,

> Abbotsinch (Glasgow) and Turnhouse (Edinburgh) will only be
> available for North Atlantic planeload charter air services when
> special permission is granted by the relevant United Kingdom
> authorities.
>
> If either airport becomes available for long-haul services, it will
> become available to both scheduled and charter services on a
> non-discriminatory basis.

This too was an important discovery and those supporting the
campaign used it to put pressure on the Government. Open Skies
had powerful supporters in the CBI, BAA, Chambers of Commerce, and the airlines. Michael Kelly, the former Lord Provost of
Glasgow was also involved as adviser to Air 2000, who sought to
operate direct flights from Glasgow to Florida. They took the
practical step of challenging the Government's policy in the Court
of Session, and won.

Air 2000 demonstrated the absurdity of the government's
policy when they were allowed to fly to America from Glasgow

or Edinburgh but only if they touched down at Prestwick, thus offering a technical opportunity for passengers to join the flight at the Ayrshire airport.

The force of the argument won the debate. I co-operated closely with Glasgow, Eastwood and Renfrew district authorities. The business communities were organised and threw their full weight behind the campaign while Strathclyde University's academics completed a major survey which highlighted the harm that was being done to the economy.

Other than the Ayrshire interests who were opposed to what we were trying to do, the only local authority who opposed strongly the opening up of Glasgow airport was Bearsden and Milngavie who were worried about the increase in noise from aircraft flying overhead as they approached the airport.

The *Landing Right* booklet pointed out that the traffic movement at Glasgow Airport was 85,000 and that even if all transatlantic flights were to transfer to Glasgow it would only add around 5 per cent to this figure. Even if the open sky policy led to a dramatic expansion in transatlantic travel the increase would only amount to a total of 10 per cent. Eventually the Government saw sense and Cecil Parkinson when he was Transport Minister lifted the restrictions.

The result of allowing market forces to decide what airports airlines would use for their different routes, I believe, has benefited everyone. I always argued that the monopoly was doing Prestwick no good, and of course never argued that airlines should be forced to fly from Glasgow. My position was, give the airlines the choice.

Prestwick aiport is now run by its own management who are operating the airport to its real strengths and it is now working out its own future. Although Manchester had a head start because of the situation that had prevailed for too long, Glasgow airport has expanded very significantly.

Glasgow is now called Glasgow International Airport and is by far the biggest economic asset Renfrewshire has. Airports are the railway stations of the twentieth century. Economic activity builds up around them and this will increasingly be the case as we move towards the millenium.

Needless to say I am delighted with what has happened since the campaign succeeded. There have been hiccups in the number of flights using Glasgow but over the longer term I am confident that Glasgow airport will benefit from its international status. Although there needs to be a rail link to Glasgow airport from the city via Paisley, it is already recognised as one of Europe's hub airports.

The success of the open airways campaign gave me a great deal of satisfaction and meant that I maintained a high profile in the Scottish media. The press in Scotland however, did not notice my 'other' campaign which was to reform the licencing laws of England and Wales.

The opportunity to contribute towards this reform arrived when I came eighth in the ballot for private members bills in October 1986. This position in the ballot did not guarantee I would have time to move any bill I proposed but there was a chance that I would get time.

You may wonder what a Scottish MP was doing attempting to liberalise the licensing laws England and Wales? It began because I was sharing a room with Rob Hayward, MP for Bristol. He told me that he believed that the licensing hours had to be liberalised and of course the new hours introduced in Scotland had been a success. Rob suggested that if a Scottish MP argued the case that liberal hours would decrease the number of cases of people taking excess alcohol then it would be more likely to be successful. Scotland already enjoyed liberal hours and had witnessed the results.

I agreed to adopt this cause for three basic reasons. It was to begin with a very unionist action to take, as it asserted the right of an MP representing a Scottish constituency to put forward legislation affecting England and Wales.

I also recalled from my student days when I observed the 'ten o'clock swill' when after I had finished working in the University Library, I would go for a beer and see groups of say four men each ordering a round at the same time before the final bell went and they would have a line up of pints sitting before them. The move was also in line with my belief that you should give people more choice.

Clement Freud, the Liberal MP was one of my supporters as were the northern MPs, mainly Labour who came from the tradition of working men's clubs.

The bill achieved its second reading and committee stage in the Commons but then the 1987 General Election intervened in March.

If we had had time the bill would have gone through, but we had won the war. We had changed the climate of thinking and when the Conservatives were returned, the Government introduced its own bill to liberalise the licensing laws south of the border.

Free market principles should apply to licensing hours but there have to be some controls to protect local residents as public houses can create a nuisance as customers leave them at night. Also there may be police views that have to be taken into account if a public house becomes a meeting place for criminal elements.

The present system appears to be working reasonably well. We are moving towards the Continental approach where families can gather and children can be present. We are also moving away from the concept that you must drink alcohol if you are in licensed premises. Many more people have a coffee or soft drink when they visit a lounge or bar and the introduction of bar meals brought with it a change of attitude. You can see the changes in places such as Leith waterfront where bistro style establishments are flourishing.

## CHAPTER 7

# RETURN TO OFFICE

When I resigned from the Scottish Office in September 1986 I told Susie that I would never again agree to become a Government Minister, and I meant it.

The EIS teachers' dispute had put me through a great deal of mental anguish. It had been an extremely difficult period partly because I knew the teachers had something of a case. I was concerned about their workload, not only because of what the union was saying but also what individual teachers in my own constituency were telling me, yet I was having to take a strong line because the Government could not concede to the targetting by the EIS of schools in Ministers' constituencies for industrial action.

Circumstances changed following John Major's election as

Conservative Party Leader in November, 1990. I had been a Margaret Thatcher supporter but this did not mean that I was anti-Michael Heseltine. Rather I was pro-Thatcher.

During the leadership campaign I was worried about how Margaret's campaign was going and spoke to George Younger about it. I was picking up bad vibes in the Commons and I heard mutterings of discontent among MPs.

One of the problems was that Margaret's campaign managers George Younger, Peter Morrison and John Moore were all senior people. She should have had more junior people involved in her campaign, people who were in touch with rank and file MPs.

Margaret achieved a majority in the first ballot but just failed by two to reach the number required to avoid a second ballot. People began to panic and Margaret made a big mistake by being in Paris when the result was announced. People began to say that they should have a choice and this was before Margaret had said she was not standing. After she had met all the members of her Cabinet her position was very difficult. She knew that she did not have the full support of her Ministers.

She made a fantastic speech in the Commons following her decision to stand down and Dennis Skinner, who is a great parliamentarian made a wonderful intervention.

Someone asked Margaret Thatcher about a European Central Bank. Quick as a flash Dennis shouted, "She'll be the Governor!" Just as quick Margaret retorted, "What a good idea!" Such wonderful parliamentary theatre reduced the tension of an emotion charged occasion.

Following Margaret Thatcher's resignation I consulted with my constituency executive before deciding who to vote for. I finally decided to support John Major after looking closely at all the candidates. I did consider Douglas Hurd who was a brilliant Foreign Secretary but perhaps not in touch enough with domestic policy to be Prime Minister. I also thought about Michael Heseltine who had been very good when he came Scotland for byelections but I thought the Party had to look to the future. I had no grudge against Michael Heseltine for standing against Margaret. He was fully entitled to stand.

After taking over the Premiership John Major reshuffled the Cabinet and moved Malcolm Rifkind from being Secretary of State for Scotland to become Defence Secretary with Ian Lang taking over as Secretary of State for Scotland.

Although I had voted for John Major, I was not a member of his campaign team. I had known John for a long time, dating back to my time in London with the CBI which meant that when he rang me at home to ask me to join the team at the Scottish Office, I could not say no.

The call which came from the Prime Minister on St Andrew's Day 1990 had not been entirely unexpected. *The Herald* had speculated that the Prime Minister would offer me a position at the Scottish Office. When he phoned me at home John said simply, "I know what you are going to say but will you do me a personal favour and come into the Government at the Scottish Office?" Having known him for so long I could not refuse.

It was arranged that an official car would come to pick me up at home to take me through to Edinburgh to meet Ian Lang. I was almost late for the meeting because the driver knew me from my previous spell in Government office, and told everyone that he knew where I stayed. Unknown to him I had moved. I no longer lived in Dumbreck but had moved to Neilston.

During my meeting with Ian Lang I explained that I was happy to be part of his team in any capacity except education! I was given responsibility for local government and industry.

It all happened very quickly. The call from John Major had come in the morning and by late afternoon the same day I was posing with Ian Lang and the rest of the Scottish Office ministerial team for press photographers.

I did not have long to settle into my new responsibilities as by February 1991, I had to deal with the imminent closure of Scotland's major steel works at Ravenscraig. The writing had been on the wall for some time which meant that when the closure announcement was made it was not as dramatic as say, that of the Linwood car plant's closure. Nevertheless there was a real danger that Lanarkshire would suffer a vicious downward cycle in the local economy and plummet into an economic dark hole

Ian Lang went to see John Major who understood the problem and who agreed that additional resources should be made available to the area. The Prime Minister asked me to chair a Lanarkshire Working Party which was formed of all the local bodies and the Lanarkshire Development Agency. We set about creating an enterprise zone and improving the infrastructure so that we could attract new industries.

The Government made an additional £15 million available to the Lanarkshire Development Agency, and British Steel put in £10 million to help towards regeneration.

I have been delighted at the progress the LDA and others have made in regenerating the local economy. The Mossend freight terminal will prove to be a hub around which the wheels of industry will turn, and of course there is the Chungwa Picture Tube Company which will create 3,000 jobs.

The arrival of the Taiwanese company is a major boost to the area, and was a reward for the work being put in by Locate in Scotland, and also for the policies the Government had been pursuing which makes the United Kingdom, and Scotland in particular, attractive to inward investors.

I was only the second Government minister to visit Taiwan. Only John Redwood had been to Taiwan before my visit and I would hope that by establishing contact between the Scottish Office at ministerial level and the Taiwan authorities I played my small part in attracting Chungwa to Scotland.

There was nothing we could really do to save Ravenscraig. The key decisions which eventually brought about its closure had been taken a long time before the closure date of April 5, 1991 when British Steel decided to invest heavily in their Welsh steel plants.

There was heavy investment in Wales over a period of time. I had argued publicly when British Steel was being privatised that it should be split in two and that Ravenscraig, Shotton and Dalzell should be made into a separate company and sold off independently. These three sites could have made steel products from start to finish. This would have given the management of that company the opportunity to make their own decisions in the best interests of Ravenscraig, Shotton and Dalzell.

I always was supicious of British Steel when it came to the question of dealing with enquiries from parties interested in buying Ravenscraig. Their interest seemed to be served by closing Ravenscraig rather than selling it to a competitor. I suspected that British Steel could be doing deals with their European counterparts so that they all kept their share of the market.

We never quite knew what was happening in relation to the approaches made by other companies as we were not the sellers. The approach by a Korean company attracted a great deal of media attention and although they talked to the Scottish Office, I had doubts about their intentions as to whether it was really about producing steel in Scotland or in fact asset stripping.

Ravenscraig was really the last of the heavy industrial plants which had been brought to Scotland in the sixties to close. Plants such as Leyland at Bathgate, the Invergordon aluminium smelter and the Linwood car factory had all closed. Some of these had only come to Scotland with their arms twisted up their backs which is an extremely unhealthy starting point.

The great irony if you look at these industrial closures is that the factories were all established under Tory Governments. Although at the time I would probably have supported the Government initiatives to bring these industrial developments to Scotland, looking back it was a disastrous policy.

The theory was that if you brought large industrial complexes to an area the suppliers would follow. But that never happened.

I of course had personal experiences of dealing with the Linwood closure as the factory was in my constituency. Almost 5,000 jobs were lost at Linwood when Talbot closed the plant. I met George Younger who was Secretary of State for Scotland at the time and Alex Fletcher who had responsibility for industry at the Scottish Office. I also met the shop stewards and attended a mass meeting of the workforce, but I eventually realised that nothing could be done to save the factory.

George Younger told me at the time that when he asked the management what it would it take to keep the plant open, they told him that the Governement would have to buy all the cars the factory produced.

I told the Commons that the Linwood was a cautionary tale for politicians of all parties saying that Rootes had been pushed into Linwood against the company's better judgement. I pointed out that Linwood had made a loss under three owners and six Prime Ministers.

My stance was not very popular and naturally the shop stewards disagreed with me but I did urge the Government to ask Nissan the Japanese car manufacturer who were known to be looking a for a suitable site in the United Kingdom to consider Linwood.

Alex Fletcher agreed to approach the company but did not hold out great hopes of success as Nissan was looking for a greenfield site. Unfortunately we now know Nissan went elsewhere.

Thankfully not all industrial sagas have a sad ending and I was delighted when the workforce at Armitage Shanks won their fight to keep their plant alive. I was absolutely convinced of their case right from the start when in January, 1992 the parent company announced the closure of the factory.

After the closure of the Barrhead factory in my own constituency, the 111 strong workforce refused to give up and they attracted the support of Sir Albert McQuarrie who led their fight.

Following a year long struggle they achieved their aim, and Barrhead Sanitaryware rose from the ashes. The workers formed a co-operative and each of those involved in the fight to retain the ceramic industry in the area put in £1,000 of their own money. I had not hesitation in putting in £1,000 to demonstrate my support for their cause.

The fight to retain the ceramic industry in the area threw up some strange moments. I spoke to Margaret Thatcher about the workers' case and she agreed to write a letter to the management asking them to delay closing the factory to give the workforce the opportunity to put a proper bid in for the plant. I, of course, was not very popular with the senior management in England because of the stance I had taken in support of the men and women in the factory and when I arrived at the gates with the letter from the Prime Minister in my pocket the security men at the gate refused to allow me through.

They were under instructions from the management not to let me in. I was still refused entry when I explained that I had a letter from the Prime Minister to deliver and I had to arrange to meet the shop stewards later in a local social club.

The campaign to save the factory included the traditional demonstration, and led to myself and Sir Albert McQuarrie walking at the front of the marchers behind the Union banners alongside the shop stewards. It was a new experience for me, and possibly for Sir Albert who, when he was Conservative MP for Banff & Buchan, was know as the Buchan Bulldog.

Old habits die hard, and soon the usual chant which normally accompanied such trade union demonstrations went up. "Maggie, Maggie Maggie, Out, Out Out!" There were some embarrassed looks on the faces of the stewards, and a local Labour councillor hurried to the back of the march to remind them of our presence and of our support.

The workers raised £2 million in their year-long fight and I was delighted when I was asked to open their new factory in Hillington in July 1993. Since then the factory has had its problems, but no one can take away from the workers their magnificent fight, and although they have now been taken over by another company a good number of jobs were secured.

In addition to my responsibilities for industry I also had local government in my portfolio, and I was asked to continue with these responsibilities following the April 1992 General Election.

In October following our election victory, we announced our plans for local government reform and there was a tremendous demand for our document from the public which indicated the great interest in what we were proposing.

The proposals had already generated a great deal of political heat and our opponents were hurling insulting accusations towards us about gerrymandering. But the simple truth is that we had a manifesto commitment to introduce a single tier system of local government in Scotland. It was also true that every Scottish political party had supported a single tier of local government at some point, although in some cases it was linked to a Scottish Parliament.

There was a touch of irony in my having the responsibility of guiding the proposed local government changes through Parliament as I had been one of only seven people who had voted against a call for local government reform at our Scottish conference.

The burden was heavier than usual because I had to take the Bill through Committee as they met on Thursday mornings and Ian Lang had to attend Cabinet meetings at that time. We only had a majority of one on the committee as Labour refused to pair Ian Lang which meant that our meetings could be fairly tense. Many people were concerned about boundaries and I agreed that I would meet any delegation that was led by an MP. The fact that an MP was leading a delegation did not necessarily mean that the MP agreed with the delegation's view, but as an MP he would believe that they had a right to have their point of view heard. I met thirty delegations from local councils to hear their views on reorganisation.

A great deal of heat was generated over the local government reforms. The opposition parties were jumping up and down accusing the Government of gerrymandering the boundaries to suit ourselves. They made great play of the fact that there had been an independent commission appointed in England to carry out this task, but they failed to point out that in Wales the exercise was carried out in a similar fashion to how we proposed to do it.

The choices in Scotland were relatively straightforward and we took the view that at the end of the day the Government has to make the decision anyway. People conveniently forget that Lord Wheatley's recommendations in the 1973–74 reorganisation were substantially changed in Parliament.

To counter the allegations of gerrymandering I was keen to avoid the guillotine, which is a parliamentary device to time limit discussion. I did not want to be accused of preventing discussion on the Government's proposals. Understandably George Robertson, Labour's Shadow Secretary of State, was also keen to avoid the guillotine.

I adopted the straightforward tactic in committee of presenting the Government's map of local authority areas and explained that we were not going to propose any changes to our own map. This meant that if the opposition parties did not like our proposals they had to come forward with their own ideas. We put forward the proposal that the existing structure of nine regions and fifty three district councils would be replaced by twenty eight single-tier authorities.

The record shows that we were prepared to listen. We spent over 170 hours in Committee, which was longer than the time it took for the Act to join the Common Market to go through its committee stages. We also agreed to a number of boundary changes in Renfrewshire, Ayrshire, Berwick and the Borders, Kincardine and Central. We came under a great deal of criticism for breaking up Strathclyde Region, but as it made up half of Scotland, I did not believe that an area this size can be truly described as local government.

I have consistently argued for small local authorities. The argument that we were throwing away Strathclyde muscle within Europe does not hold water. The East of Scotland authorities had got together for Europe and I see no reason why this should not happen with the new unitary authorities if they so decide.

The Convention of Scottish Local Authorities made what I believe was a bad error of judgement when they decided on a policy of non co-operation. We still received the messages through various channels. It was not a policy which was going to succeed.

George Robertson came to the Committee with a justifiably high reputation following his handling of Labour's tactics during the debates on the Maastricht Treaty. But he stated publicly he expected English Tory rebels on the Local Government Bill so it could be defeated. That belief probably prolonged local government opposition to the bill. In practice I knew there would be no opposition from English colleagues except on points of detail. Many English backbenchers told me privately they admired the way we were handling reorganisation in Scotland compared to the much more complex procedure south of the border.

Our opponents in Parliament tried to make a great play about Eastwood District. The fact is that the boundaries are exactly the same as the Parliamentary boundaries, and there is no doubt that the majority of people in the area wanted to stay out of Glasgow. We had suggested that Ralston should be included in the new unitary authority as it had previously been within the parliamentary boundaries but it became obvious that there was a majority in Ralston who wanted to stay attached to Paisley, and we accepted this change. Eastwood is, in my mind, a well balanced authority, with an industrial area around Barrhead as well as residential areas in the rest of the district.

Certainly my return to Ministerial office had proved more than a little interesting. I felt much more relaxed second time around and was comfortable with my portfolio. I had my previous experience under my belt, and although I worked long hours, there was no real strain.

## CHAPTER 8

# A WALK ON THE MOTORWAY

Before turning to the circumstances surrounding my resignation in February 1995, it is worth reiterating the crucial importance of the M77 extension. I had long campaigned for it and knew that internal objective Scottish Office analyses showed the M77 to be Scotland's most needed road improvement in terms of reducing congestion and delays and improving road safety.

Shortly after my resignation I set out the arguments for the road. The following quotation from the article I wrote in the *Scottish Daily Mail* (February 10th, 1995) summarised these:

> The motorway south from the centre of Glasgow through the city and my constituency of Eastwood stops very quickly.

Beyond there, huge numbers of people every day have to drive through a variety of suburban roads.

None of these roads were built for the traffic volumes now being carried. The implications of this in terms of congestion, delay, noise and accidents are clearly obvious.

Certainly it is crucial for the economic and environmental future of the Eastwood constituency. Without the road, the companies in industrial areas such as Barrhead will not have reasonable access to the Central Scotland motorway network. That is significant for them – they must be competitive in time and access. More generally, without the M77 extension, Eastwood and the whole of the south side of Glasgow will become one huge traffic jam.

Eastwood is an area of growth. Without the new road, the residents of more and more quiet residential streets will have to suffer queues of cars, vans and lorries trying to get to and from Ayrshire and Glasgow.

The M77 extension is not only about the reasonable rights of people in quiet streets to live without unnecessary traffic. It is also about lives.

Questions asked by Ayrshire MPs have shown the present road system to be the most dangerous in Scotland. That must stop – and as soon as possible.

Every Ayrshire MP, irrespective of party, is a committed supporter of the Ayr Road Route. They all know how important it is for the safety and well-being of their constituents.

Labour controlled Strathclyde Regional Council wants the road. So do all the other local authorities involved. So does the European Community. So does the Government. The new road has been planned, the route known for many years.

Who then is against the road? Not the local people. Not any of the political parties. But there is a group. I have met them in my constituency. Not one was a constituent. They have their agenda – and it is nothing to do with the interests of my constituents.

The incident in the grounds around the Pollok Castle Estate in the constituency which led to my resignation as a Minister was extremely short. It was over quickly but it filled the columns of many newspapers for days.

At first, to be truthful, I thought it would be quickly forgotten about even after I had read the Scottish press. Most people at this juncture seemed to think it was a bit of a joke. After all no one had been hurt in what was little more than a bit of a melee.

A protest had developed and a number of people had set up a camp in the woods at Pollok in direct oppostion to the planned route of the new motorway. In setting up their main camp – the so-called Pollok Free State – they had attracted considerable publicity. I went along to the area in my own constituency to see for myself what was happening.

The reason for my visit at that particular time was that I was due to see Ian Lang later that week to express to him the views of constituents who had written to me on the subject. Scottish Ministers had already met to discuss this.

I had a particular problem as a number of constituents working on the site felling the trees told me there had been a number of threats made to them. I felt I had to do something about this and informed my fellow Ministers that I intended to visit the sites. The actual site I visited was not the so-called Pollok Free State but an area in my constituency where work was being carried out.

I was concerned by the fact that none of the protestors were my constituents, although I know from experience that there are plenty of people in Eastwood who protest, having come across them at various demonstrations. There have never been any problems between us. There is no doubt that some of those involved in the M77 protests were what I would describe as 'professional protestors' and they came from all over the world to join in the action. It was not my intention to meet the protestors when I visited Pollok Castle Estate.

However shortly after we arrived at the protestors' sub-camp in Stewarton Road near Newton Mearns we were confronted by a group of the protestors and when we tried to return to our car our path was blocked.

There was a lot of pushing and shoving going on but it calmed down and we left the scene. The incident was well covered by the Scottish press, but it would have been largely forgotten about by the end of that week, and the Scottish media would have moved on to the next story.

The situation changed when the English press picked up the story and began to build it up into a major issue. The incident followed a number of Ministerial scandals which had eventually led to a number of resignations. The Prime Minister had said publicly that Ministers who faced problems should consider their position. In light of this statement I believed it only proper that I should consider my position.

I talked it over with Adrian Shinwell, a constituent and my solicitor who is also a personal friend, when it became obvious that the whole episode was being built up into a yet another problem for the Prime Minister caused by a Government Minister.

On the Tuesday morning I spoke to the then Chief Whip, Richard Ryder, and told him, "Richard, I am going to resign, as this will run and run, and people will start to question the Prime Minister." I told him that I was resigning on the grounds that I did not wish to cause any embarrassment to the Government.

I then wrote my letter of resignation and showed it to Ian Lang. I told Ian that my mind was made up. I then sent the letter to the Prime Minister.

Dated 7 February 1995, I wrote,

> Dear Prime Minister, You will have seen the publicity surrounding my visit on Sunday to a site in my constituency. I was there solely as the Member of Parliament for Eastwood.
>
> However I do not wish in any way to be an embarrassment to a Government I have been proud to serve. Having discussed the matter with my family I believe it only right that I resign and now wish to do so.
>
> It has been a great privilege to have been a member of your Government and in particular to have worked with Ian and other friends in the Scottish Office. It goes without saying that you, Ian and this Conservative and Unionist Government will

have the continuing committed support of the Member of
Parliament for Eastwood.

John Major sent an understanding letter in reply which said:

> Thank you for your letter about your decision to stand down
> from the Government. I was sorry to hear the news but I do
> understand and appreciate your reasons for doing so. You have
> provided great service to the Scottish Office and the
> Government over many years. I am particularly grateful for the
> skillful way you helped pilot the Local Government (Scotland)
> Bill through the House last session, and for the effective and
> tireless way you have campaigned for the Government's case in
> Scotland.
>
> As Industry Minister over the past four years you have made
> an important contribution to the policies which have
> underpinned Scotland's continuing economic progress.
>
> Thank you also for your characteristically generous comments
> about your support for the Government from the back benches.
>
> Norma joins me in sending our best wishes to you and Susie.

I also issued a statement to the media explaining why I had
resigned. The statement read:

> I have today resigned from the Government. It is a Government
> which I am proud to have served and I take to the back benches
> many happy memories of my time at the Scottish Office.
>
> I have, however, explained to the Prime Minister and to the
> Secretary of State for Scotland that recent allegations made by
> individuals opposed to the extension to the M77 must be
> answered. There have been wild and inaccurate allegations. But
> they related to my conduct as an individual and I do not wish
> my Government to become involved or to be deflected in any
> way from issues of greater concern.
> I hope that my resignation will ease the considerable stress
> placed on me and on my family in recent days and that, being
> relieved of the duties of government will afford me the time
> and opportunity to defend myself to the full. I intend to do so
> as an individual and as the Member of Parliament for Eastwood

whose constituents I have been privileged to represent for fifteen years.

I have written to the Prime Minister and to the Secretary of State expressing my regret for any embarrassment that these allegations my have caused them and to the Government and assuring them of my continuing loyalty and support. For the present, I shall have nothing to add to this statement.

The media of course ignored the last sentence and I found them congregating on the pavement outside my London flat. I realised that there was no point in ignoring this so I went downstairs to meet them.

I was asked what I planned to do now that I was no longer a Government minister to which I replied, "I am going to now walk to my office which will better for my health than the Ministerial car." This answer lightened the atmosphere and was the line most of the popular press picked up the following morning.

There was also a bit of humour in the House when a Labour MP told me that I had created a record as I was the only Minister to resign without anyone asking for my resignation. This was true. No one had.

Most of what happened on that day has been well documented but what was often forgotten in the torrent of words written about my visit with members of my constituency, the sub contractor responsible for removing the trees and my son is that on the day I was neither warned nor charged. I went voluntarily to the police station.

I was extremely surprised that I was eventually charged. It was a Crown Office decision to charge me and not one made by the local fiscal.

News of the charge did not come until nine weeks after the incident, April 13, on the eve of a visit to Libya to meet Col Gadaffi regarding the two suspects whom the Crown Office wanted to come to Scotland to stand trial for the Lockerbie bombing atrocity.

I denied the original charge because I was not guilty of it. I did not brandish a pickaxe. I could not have brandished the pick axe even if I had wanted to as I suffer from arthritis and would not have been able to lift it above shoulder height.

I later changed my plea to guilty after the fiscal altered the charge to 'presenting' the pick axe. This was true. I had held it in front of me but not in a threatening manner.

I also admit that I was shouting, but so were a large number of other people. There was a lot of pushing and shoving going on, but I was the only one charged. The fiscal agreed to change the charge only at the last minute, the Friday before I was due to appear at Paisley Sheriff Court on the Monday.

My legal advisers had intimated to the authorities that I would plead guilty if the charged was altered to 'present' rather than brandish. The entire affair placed a great deal of pressure on my family. Susie was a tower of strength. She supported me absolutely throughout the whole difficult period. Some hurtful things were said in the media but as a politician you have to be able to withstand these pressures. It is different when your family becomes involved.

I was also immensely grateful for the large number of letters of support I received from my constituents and members of the Eastwood Conservative Association whose chairman then was Cliff Hargreaves and agent Anne McFadden. They were both extremely supportive, as was the Party generally. So were neighbours in Neilston and in Kennington – according to London journalists who interviewed people in the street and in the pub next to my flat – the famous Cricketers.

But perhaps I most appreciated the way in which my political opponents dealt with the whole matter. Neither the Labour Party nor the SNP and Liberal Democrats tried to score political points from the affair, and many of those I had exchanged words with across the floor of the House of Commons offered me words of sympathy and support.

I have been asked many times since if I miss being a Minister. Of course I miss the opportunity to influence decisions in the way that a Minister can, but I was never fanatical about being a Government Minister. Being MP for Eastwood is the greatest privilege and I have always enjoyed my constituency work and involvement in local issues on behalf of ordinary people. That is why I stand for election.

CHAPTER 9

# DEFENDING THE UNION

Although as I have explained earlier my parents were not active in politics, I was brought up in a Liberal Unionist household. When the Liberal Party split over the Irish Question their families had chosen the side which believed in the Union between Northern Ireland and the rest of the United Kingdom.

During my childhood and early teenage years the Union between Scotland and England was, perhaps wrongly, taken for granted. In more recent times the debate over the Act of Union between Scotland and England came to the fore following Labour's defeat in the Hamilton byelection at the hands of the SNP's Winnie Ewing. The Scottish National Party bandwagon started to roll and the Nationalists started to gain parliamentary seats.

The Conservative Party of course maintained a Unionist position but many in the party felt that some initiative should be taken. I did not publicly criticise Prime Minister, Ted Heath when he made his Declaration of Perth. He proposed a Scottish Assembly without any economic powers.

I was at the time, both young and a new candidate, and it is fair to say I had not thought through my views on the subject in enough detail to allow me to question the Party's leadership.

My views on the constitutional issue firmed up during my time as Director of the CBI in Scotland when most members of the CBI were strong supporters of the Scotland Says No campaign in the run up to the 1979 referendum on a Scottish Assembly.

It was at this time that I really began to think hard about the issue, and came down firmly on the side of maintaining the Union. Having said this, I should immediately say that I am not fanatically anti-independence.

I recall that during the television debate between George Robertson and Alex Salmond, that when asked to give a second preference between the three choices independence, devolution and status quo, George Robertson refused to give his second preference. I have stated my second preference clearly on several occasions and it would be for independence.

The Callaghan Government was brought down by its failure to get the Scotland Act through Parliament following the March 1979 Referendum, and I made my Maiden Speech on the question of devolution during the repeal of the Scotland Act debate.

Seventeen years have passed since I rose in Parliament as a raw recruit to the Commons to make my speech but my views have not changed on the subject in the intervening years. It is, I believe, worth placing on record what I said at that time. I spoke for ten minutes and my introduction followed the traditional pattern laid down for Maiden Speeches as I described to the House my constituency. I then came to the meat of my speech saying:

> It is perhaps particularly appropriate that in this Maiden
> Speech Betty Harvie Anderson's successor should support the

repeal of the Scotland Act because no one could have worked to oppose the Act with greater vigour, determination and conviction than she.

We must now look ahead. Firstly, can we learn any lessons from the failure of the Act to receive anything like the level of popular support that its proponents expected? I should like to make two points.

First, the campaign for the Act suffered from a fatal flaw. The Rt Hon Member for Glasgow Craigton (Bruce Millan) and his colleagues argued for the Act on, broadly speaking, two grounds, that it was a reasonable and sensible reform of government, and that this sort of devolution would halt the move to independence.

The Scottish National Party argued with great conviction precisely the opposite. It argued that people should vote for the Act on the grounds that it would be the first step to independence. In looking ahead, the first point that arises from the referendum debate is that we must always ask where any change will lead in the long term.

Secondly I should like to refer to the role of the business community. Renfrewshire East has a large number of business men and the business community was strongly opposed to the Scotland Act, a fact that was often not understood by the supporters of the Act. There was an amazing campaign during the referendum about who financed Scotland Says No. It was first suggested that the campaign was being financed by the English. At one point, even the CBI was accused of financing it – though that was clearly absurd.

Next we were told that faceless multinationals were financing the campaign, then it was alleged to be Dutch land speculators, and after that Arab land speculators. The only traditional bogeymen who were not mentioned as financing the campaign were the CIA and the South African secret service.

The fact is that the Scotland Says No campaign was financed by Scottish businessmen, large and small because of their grave concern about the implications of the Act for investment and jobs. In looking ahead, we must look to the effects of any changes on Scotland's wealth creators – the business community.

I support the line taken by my Right Hon Friend the Secretary of State in regard to all-party talks. Of his four options, I am attracted, as he is, to the route of stronger Select Committees. I do not support the simple status quo, but there are strong arguments for it. It commands at least substantial minority support in Scotland, as the opinion polls on the subject have indicated. It may be that the status quo has more support in Scotland than any other option. It is arguable that it has the support of perhaps more than 50 per cent of those who vote Conservative as well as support in other parties.

The General Election certainly showed no manifest desire in Scotland for radical change. Seven of my Hon Friends gained seats from the SNP. On the Labour side, the views of the Hon Member for West Lothian (Tam Dalyell) on devolution were well known and he increased his majority from about 2,000 to about 21,000.

In addition although we wish the all-party talks well, it may be that there will not be agreement between the parties. In that case we shall retain the status quo.

My main point is that the onus of proof is on the advocates of change. It is argued that there are substantial imperfections in the government of Scotland, but evidence of imperfection is not, in itself justification for change. If we advocate a change we must prove that it would be a positive improvement. We are justified in having change only if there is broad support for it. It would be pointless for the Government to present to the House a scheme that was opposed by the overwhelming majority of Opposition Members. We would be back playing the Scotland Act, with the parties reversed.

In conclusion, I thank Hon Members on both sides for hearing my first speech in the customary polite silence – more or less. In fully supporting Government policy, I suggest that we should proceed with care and caution. If there is to be change, we should proceed to it only on the basis of a much wider consensus of support, both inside and outside the House, than the Scotland Act ever received.

The conditions I laid down for change have never been met. There is no broad consensus and I believe that what is presently proposed by the Scottish Constitutional Convention, which Labour and the Liberal Democrats support, is unworkable.

If what was on offer was a serious federal system covering the entire United Kingdom, I might not like the idea, but it could work. I do not accept the suggestion that we can somehow count the number of votes cast for Labour and Liberal Democrats in the last General Election and claim that all these voters support the proposed devolution plans. It is absurd to claim this.

Neither do I accept opinion polls as a true reflection of the Scottish public's real attitude towards devolution. Certainly if you ask people in an opinion poll if they are in favour of a Scottish Parliament a high percentage say yes. The problem arises when you come down to the precise proposals. The results are different when detailed proposals are discussed.

People in Scotland who support devolution within the United Kingdom constantly forget how the people in England would react to the proposal. I do not believe that England would tolerate the West Lothian question which simply is, why should Scottish MPs in Parliament be allowed to vote on matters which affect only England and Wales when English and Welsh representatives will have no say in Scottish legislation?

To be fair to the Scottish Liberal Democrats they realise this, which is why they say there should be fewer Scottish MPs in Westminster if a Scottish Parliament was established, and that there would be no need for a Scottish Secretary of State. The Liberals however, are really federalists.

The same cannot be said for the Labour Party. They have abandoned their federal-type proposals for England and Wales and what they are now suggesting for the remainder of the UK is in no way on a level with their devolution plans for Scotland.

Regardless of the West Lothian question I do not believe that Labour's proposals are right for Scotland. I have no doubt that the Callaghan Government's interest in devolution was motivated by the rise of the SNP in the 1970s, and of course in Opposition the concept of a Scottish Parliament has considerable advantages. It is the convenient answer to every grievance, real or imagined.

There can be few social or economic problems for which devolution has not been put forward as a solution. The reality is that a Scottish Parliament would impose real costs on Scotland without resolving any of our problems. There is the obvious cost of setting up a Parliament and the 129 members would have to be paid for.

During the period that Westminster was debating the issue and also during the time that elections were being held for the new body there would be a period of great uncertainty. This would hit companies already operating in Scotland, and bodies such as Locate in Scotland, even if they were still operating, would find it extremely difficult to attract foreign investment to this country. Business does not like uncertainty and a Scottish Parliament would create a great deal of uncertainty over a period of several years during which times a lot of damage could be done to the Scottish economy.

Great claims have been made about how a Scottish Parliament would solve all our problems and unsullied by experience it has been a convenient answer for Government critics. The hard reality is that it could not change the economic facts of life. Changing our constitution would not alter the world markets for the goods we export such as personal computers or whisky.

Neither would a Scottish Parliament convince Europe that Edinburgh should be the financial investment centre of Europe. The proposed body in Edinburgh would not be able to magically produce better houses, faster roads or anything else. They would all have to be paid for.

Labour-controlled local authorities in Scotland have proved how their party thinks problems should be solved by throwing money at them, but where would the extra money come from? There are only three possible sources, the Treasury, or the Tartan Tax, or business rates at local level.

We can discount any thoughts people might harbour that the money would come from the Treasury. Public spending per head in Scotland has been consistently higher than in England. This additional allocation has come about partly because of the influence a Scottish Secretary of State for Scotland exerts in the Cabinet, but it would be highly unlikely that a British Government could sustain the argument that the Scots should have their own representative in the Cabinet in addition to having their own Parliament. Indeed it is likely that pressure would be applied by MPs from other parts of the UK that spending per head should be at least equalised.

If the additional money is not forthcoming from the Treasury then that would leave the Tartan Tax as the only means of raising additional revenue.

There would be constant friction with the Scottish Parliament who would no doubt use Westminster as an easy excuse for any problems the Scottish economy was having. And there would be a steady stream of demands for additional resources to be allocated to Scotland, or more powers to be given Edinburgh. This situation would lead to frustration and disenchantment as the imperfections of an imperfect system became clear.

The SNP would thrive in these conditions and would quickly become the vehicle of protest. One only has to study what has happened to foresee the outcome. The SNP would argue that the only real solution to Scotland's problems was independence.

Any Government which introduced a Scottish Parliament would have to deal with the West Lothian Question which has been raised on countless occasions by the Labour Party's own Tam Dalyell who is one of the most astute Parliamentarians sitting in the House of Commons at the present time. What happens if a Party gains the balance of power at Westminster on the strength of Scottish votes like the recent Labour Governments of 1964 and 1974? Would the English MPs whose party was forced into opposition because of Scottish votes be expected to put up with this state of affairs? It is hardly likely.

George Robertson and others on the Labour side have tried to use the situation in Northern Ireland for their own ends. They have accused the Government of being inconsistent.

The truth is that we cannot compare Northern Ireland in a number of ways – including having only eighteen MPs at Westminster to Scotland which has seventy two MPs. There is no proper local government in Ulster at present. What is proposed in reality fills that gap. Once again the Liberal Democrats have at least faced up to this problem and have said that they believe that the number of Scottish MPs would have to be reduced at Westminster if a Scottish Parliament was to be elected.

Labour refuse to recognise the logic of this argument because they are afraid that without their Scottish contingent of MPs they would never again be in a position to form a British Labour Government.

John Major was right to raise the issue of the Union right across the nation during the last General Election. It is correct to give notice that at the next General Election the electorate in other parts of the United Kingdom will be made aware of what Labour proposes for part of the UK.

General elections are usually fought on a number of fronts – as Ted Heath found to his cost in February 1974. It does seem that many in England are not particularly interested in what is seen as a purely Scottish and Welsh question. They would soon realise the problems if the current plans were later implemented. I firmly believe that as we hammer home the dangers of the Tartan Tax the people of Scotland will begin more and more to see the dangers of the Labour Party's devolution proposals.

There is no electoral threat to the Conservative Party in continuing to spell out clearly our support for the Union. My position on this question has always been very clear, and at the April 1992 General Election we succeeded in getting the largest swing against Labour in any constituency throughout the UK.

There exist within the Conservative Party in Scotland those who believe that we should adopt a devolution policy of our own. They appear to argue this from the position that such a change in policy would bring us some political gain.

The suggestion that voters would swing to the Conservatives because we were in favour of some form of Scottish Assembly is implausible. We would still be seen as being less enthusiastic than our opponents, and to put forward some half-baked scheme would be the worst of all possible worlds. It would be derided by our opponents and would appall the business community who have thought very seriously about the implications. It is no answer to suggest that we should put forward some watered down scheme which would not have the dangerous powers proposed by Labour.

If Labour's Assembly or Parliament were to be set up it would continually argue for more powers and under pressure Westminster would eventually concede, as many English MPs might take the view that any subsequent problems which arose would be down to the Scots. Conflict between the Scottish and United Kingdom Parliaments over powers and resources is inherent in the current Opposition proposals.

No, we should stand by our support of the Union because the form of Scottish Parliament or Assembly proposed would be a steep downhill, one way street with full separation at the bottom.

## CHAPTER 10

# EUROPE

My views on Europe have always been guided first and foremost by my belief in free trade. In the period leading up to the United Kingdom joining the Common Market I was strongly against it because I believed that it was basically a protectionist organisation.

This is why when I stood in the Dundee East election my campaign slogan was 'A Vote for Stewart is a Vote Against the Common Market.' However I voted Yes in the Harold Wilson referendum because Britain was already a member and it was therefore a different question. I believe that the European Union is still protectionist and should be opened up – a Europe from the Urals to the Atlantic.

Indeed I would go further. I strongly favour Malcolm

Rifkind's vision of a free trade area that also covers the North Atlantic and of course there is now a free trade area covering the United States, Canada, and Mexico.

There is a tremendous dilemma surrounding Europe. The Treaty of Rome was supposed to be about freedom of movement of goods, people and capital but for example the Common Agricultural Policy is an appalling system. It costs the average British family around £20 a week and does not do the British farmer a lot of good either. One of the consequences of this is that our taxpayers are paying European farmers to grow tobacco which is exported to Third World countries. It is completely absurd.

Margaret Thatcher did her best. During her premiership, she was not anti-European. After all she signed the Single European Act. But she was strong on handbagging the hypocrisy that surrounds the European Union. One of the driving forces behind the Treaty of Rome was to prevent further wars between Germany and France but it quickly became a case of the prosperous Western countries getting together to protect their markets.

The European Union should not be looking inwards but outwards towards Eastern Europe and across the Atlantic to North America. But the consensus among the elite of our society is that you must be nice to the Europeans, you must not be nasty. But it is pro-European to point out the defects in some of Europe's policies, and people are beginning to understand this.

It is understandable that major industrialists are in favour of a single European currency because it would be far more convenient and would reduce a company's exchange costs. Of course a company has the advantage that if they happen to be in a part of Europe which is disadvantaged by a single currency then they can move to another country or region. It is not so simple for individuals to move.

John Major's position on joining a single currency is entirely sensible. The decision need not be made at the present time. Public opinion across Europe is increasingly realising the importance of the preconditions which should arguably be tightened.

The single currency is not merely a technical agreement. The exchange rate mechanism a country can get out of, as we have already shown, but if Britain joins up to the single currency then it is for all practical purposes irreversible. We would be effectively passing economic policy to a European Central Bank. That is not just a technical economic change. To be blunt, it is about who is running the show. A single currency is workable only if the Central State can move resources around to meet economic problems.

There is no doubt in my mind that it is a constitutional question and should be put to the electorate. If I were given the opportunity to vote in a referendum at this moment in time I would vote No. Although I accept there could be a time in the future when I would vote Yes.

In theory, people can move from one part of the European Union to another but in practice it is very difficult. There are a number of practical problems involving culture and language. A British person could move to Sicily or East Germany but I am certain they would find it very difficult to find a job in either of those areas.

Some pundits have pointed to the United States as an example of how a single currency is both necessary and practical. But the Americans can move around their continent easily. They have the same language to start with, and although obviously there are regional cultural differences, the basic culture transcends the entire country.

If there is a single currency then someone must decide the exchange rate policy and there would have to be in place some kind of super state politician who would say to the Central Bank, this is our policy.

If we say Yes to a single currency we are making an irrevocable step in the direction of a European Federal State of some kind, which is far from being a mere technical point. This is why I believe that not only the consent of Parliament is needed, but also the consent of the people.

My desire is to have a larger wider Europe, rather than a deeper Europe. Indeed that really is the issue which faces politicians throughout Europe who talk of enlarging the EU. If we widen the community we cannot deepen it as fast and everyone realises this. People in Britain when using the term Europe do not include themselves unless they are using it in a geographic sense.

I am in favour of Europe which is a free market but before we can widen Europe we would have to do something about the Common Agricultural Policy (CAP). Huge subsidies go to European farmers and if we were to extend this to farmers in Eastern Europe there would be an enormous cost.

CAP is being steadily reformed but not very quickly. It is difficult to reform CAP because the farming lobby everywhere is extremely well organised, particularly in Germany and France where they are a key constituency. They also receive a high degree of support from urban areas who tend to see farmers as good solid people who are the salt of the earth.

I have first hand knowledge of the farming community in Britain as I have a farming vote in Eastwood of between 400 and 500. I meet the East Renfrewshire National Farmers Union and they are extremely sensible people who are not fanatical when it comes to subsidies. But then British farmers are very efficient.

One way round the CAP problem is to widen Europe by extending it through the free trade route. Norway for example is not a member of the European Union but it enjoys free trade. We could offer Eastern Europe free trade status as a way out of the CAP problem.

There is also a major difficulty with the EU fisheries policies. The Government is not to blame for the present situation but it is another example of how the EU is being exploited.

A strong line on fisheries is necessary. I believe we could scrap the Common Fisheries Policy (CFP) which is all about access without endangering the entire EU. If the Government announced that it planned to withdraw from the CFP I would support it. This would be a high risk strategy but it would protect our own fishing stock and our fishing industry. The Government could then use the Royal Navy to keep fishing boats from other countries out of our waters.

We need a fish preservation policy, and a policy for the

control of fishing and the CFP is an example of where the EU is going wrong.

John Major's position on Europe is receiving increasing support. There is no possibility of monetary union by 1999. The Prime Minister's arguments have been proven correct and a substantial number of the member states are now supporting the British Government's position. I don't believe that the question of a monetary union, or whether we have a referendum before taking such a step, is a party political matter.

Tony Blair and John Major are not very far apart on this question. Understandably many of those against a referendum argue that voters do not necessarily vote on the issue, but take the opportunity to express their dissatisfaction with the Government of the day, and this was a factor in the referendum on the Scotland Act when the Labour Government was not very popular at the time. The question must be very clear and it is necessary to ensure that the voters know what they are voting on.

There have been problems within the Conservative Party over Europe because people hold very strong views on this subject but the reality is that views are just as divided within the Labour Party as they are within the Tories. I certainly disagreed with the decision to withdraw the whip from the so-called Euro-rebels. I sympathised with the 'rebels' and argued in the Party that it was wrong to withdraw the whip.

Teddy Taylor, for example has held the same views on Europe for forty years. I was outraged at the whip being withdrawn from Teddy. After all everyone has known where he has stood for all these years. At the time I gave Teddy a note to say that if he needed a Government Minister to speak to his constituency party just to give me a ring. If I had been asked along to Teddy's constituency I would have told them that although I did not agree with what he had done, he is a wonderful MP.

Europe is THE issue of British politics today. It goes to the heart of our society and transcends party politics. It is an issue that everyone should have a say in, and not merely MPs in the House of Commons. I say both major parties should commit themselves to a referendum on monetary union and remove the issue from party politics.

What of the oft reiterated assertion that the arguments on a simple currency are too difficult for the ordinary people to understand? The question must be clear. But that is not a problem. For a future Government to join a Single European Currency would require an Act of Parliament. So the question on the referendum ballot paper would be simple – do you support the Euro-Currency Act? Yes or No?

Earlier this year in an article in The Herald (22 January 1996) I discussed the view that the common folk would not understand the issues:

> Quite apart from its unacceptable elitist nature the argument is nonsense. At one level the pros and cons do need to be spelt out – a recent OECD economic outlook outlined the advantages of a single currency in 20 lines but took 140 for the problems. But the key points are not technically obscure. Removing exchange rate adjustments makes cross-border trade easier which helps both businesses and tourists. Large monetary and economic unions like the United States can clearly be successful.
>
> On the other hand, being a member of a common currency is not a prerequisite for economic success. Ireland broke its currency union with the UK in 1978 and has since prospered.
>
> There should be no doubt in anyone's mind that joining a single currency is a fundamental constitutional issue. It is not simply a case of whether we use pounds or Ecus when we do our shopping. A common European currency is the first step towards a common European government.
>
> In Britain the value of the pound we all use is controlled (hopefully) by the Bank of England and the bank's policy is broadly determined by the Government which is answerable to Parliament. It would be no different if we joined a common European currency. There would have to be a common European central bank and a common European government to control it. Whether one describes this as a European Super State or sensible integration is really beside the point. The key is the fundamental and irreversible change that is implied.

## CHAPTER 11

# THE ELECTORATE—THE REAL VIPS

Understandably most of the media coverage surounding my career has centred on my activities as a Scottish Office minister. But the key job is being a constituency MP. That is what we are elected to be.

I succeeded Betty Harvie Anderson as MP in the May 1979 General Election when Margaret Thatcher first defeated Labour to become the Prime Minister. Betty had held East Renfrewshire, as the constituency was then known as, for twenty years. She became Baroness Skrimshire of Quarter after she gave up the seat but sadly she died shortly afterwards and I attended her funeral service in Dunblane Cathedral and the memorial service at Westminster.

Betty was a very popular MP as was shown by the number of constituents who attended the service. She held the distinction of being the first woman member of Parliament to sit in the Speaker's Chair when she was elected deputy speaker. In this position she was not permitted to show any political leanings and she resigned as deputy speaker in order to be able to campaign actively for a No vote in the March 1979 referendum on the setting up of a Scottish Assembly. Betty was also a close friend of Margaret Thatcher.

Although much changed by boundary reviews, the constituency has been held by the Conservatives since 1924 and I was introducing myself as a new face to the electorate and campaigned broadly along national party lines on lower income tax, tougher law and order policies and less State spending. I was delighted when in winning the seat in May 1979, we increased the Conservative majority by 4,528 to 11,500 over Labour when the constituency had an electorate of almost 68,000.

I was one of 130 'new boys' who went to Westminster following the election result and life in Westminster took a bit of getting used to. My first mistake was when I entered the members' smoking room carrying my briefcase. No one said anything to me but I was the subject of some long hard stares. It was only later that I was told that it was customary to leave briefcases and working papers outside.

One of those who came to my aid on several occasions was George Robertson who had won Hamilton in the previous year in a byelection and had got to know the place better. He turned me round on a number of occasions and pointed me in the right direction, not politically of course I should add.

My salary, as a backbencher, paid by cheque every month, was £6897 and I was allowed to claim up to £3,046 a year for accommodation, and also up to £4,200 for secretarial and office services.

I soon became aware of the wide variety of problems an MP is asked by constituents to tackle when a Polish War veteran contacted my secretary. Through the Polish ex-servicemen's organisation and the Catholic Church he had arranged to meet his mother in Italy. He had not seen his mother for many years and he had applied for a passport for the trip. He needed the passport almost immediately but it had got stuck in the system. I rang up an under-secretary at the Home Office and they tracked down the passport application. The Home Office sent a car to Croydon to pick up the passport and deliver it to me. I then flew to Glasgow and handed the passport over to the Polish ex-serviceman at Glasgow Airport while he was waiting for his flight to Italy.

It really was a baptism of fire, and I was delighted to be able to help, but thank goodness not all the problems I am asked to deal with have such a short timescale attached to them.

However I cannot claim to satisfy all my constituents all of the time. One case which taught me a lesson was when a constituent wrote complaining about a bus shelter being placed outside their home which made it difficult for them to get their car out of their driveway. I took the matter up with Strathclyde Region who proved to be very helpful and moved the bus shelter which resulted in my secretary opening forty letters of complaint from other enraged constituents. This episode taught me to check out the background to complaints before acting.

Eastwood, since it was created following the Wheatley Report, has always had a fractious relationship with Glasgow District Council who have voiced the opinion on many occasions that Eastwood should be part of the city. This opinion is not shared by the vast majority of my constituents and I have always supported Keep Eastwood Out of Glasgow campaigns.

Relationships between the two Districts reached freezing point over Rouken Glen Park which became a political issue in 1983 when Glasgow District Council voted to close the park. Although it was outside Glasgow's city boundary the park was gifted to the citizens of Glasgow in 1906 by Lord Rowallan. Glasgow's Labour administration claimed that because of Government cuts in local authority spending they could no longer keep the park open.

In fairness, the park had already been a matter of dispute

between the two districts when Eastwood in 1980 had stopped paying 12 per cent towards the running costs after a fall-out between them regarding joint properties.

The controversy had started while I was on holiday but on my return I criticised Glasgow District Council forcibly for their "political vindictiveness" for I had no doubt that they were taking this action because Rouken Glen was in a Conservative controlled district.

Rouken Glen was eventually transferred to Eastwood and it is now a prime example of how Conservative controlled councils can operate publicly owned assets in partnership with the private sector. Eastwood District Council has introduced a successful Garden Centre into the Park and also a Butterfly Kingdom, both run by private concerns.

My personal assistant Jeanette Muir deals with an average of 500 letters a week. We discuss action to be taken and referrals to be made. I also hold regular constituency surgeries to discuss particular problems face to face and make home visits to those unable to attend. My home number is in the telephone book and people also use that to contact me.

I am normally in London in the House of Commons from Monday to late on Thursday evening, but Jeanette will see people in my absence if urgent action is required and prepare a large file of letters for my signature on Fridays.

My contact with constituents keeps me in touch with public opinion, and among the issues which have resulted in a larger than usual postbag is abortion. I am pro-life and am close to the line taken by the Catholic Church. In 1980 I supported John Corrie's Private Member's Bill to reduce the time limit in which abortions could take place from 28 to 24 weeks. I have never hidden my views on this subject from the electorate, and this has resulted in people on both sides of the debate writing to me in large numbers.

If any constituent writes to me with a view with I disagree with on a particular subject then I explain politely that I differ from them. If constituents write to me raising their concerns about a current matter then I will if possible raise the subject in the House of Commons which I did, for example, on the subject of bank holidays.

The Scottish banks, it would appear, would like to see bank holidays changed to bring them into line with English bank holidays and following representations from constituents I put a question down. This is typically how a backbencher acts.

The largest number of letters I received from constituents on any single issue was in 1984 following the Domestic Rates Revaluation which had a knock-on effect on domestic rates bills. The number of letters I received on this was well into four figures and they were all individual letters, not circulars. People were very angry at the time and it was a problem I had predicted.

I had to face the voters again in June 1983 when the electorate had been reduced by around 8,000 voters to 60,264 with the removal of Ralston and Elderslie from the constituency. The constituency's name was also changed from East Renfrewshire to Eastwood.

By this time I was Minister for Home Affairs and the Environment, and although my ministerial duties carried on throughout the election campaign I tried to spend as much time as possible in the constituency.

The state of the economy was a major issue in this campaign as we had just come through a recession, but in Eastwood I gained 46.6 per cent of the vote to gather 21,072 votes, a majority over Jim Pickett, the SDP/Alliance candidate of 8,595.

I was delighted with the result and afterwards I can recall calling in at the Whitecraigs Lawn Tennis Club where I knew some of those who had supported me would be watching the election results on a giant screen the club had put in. One of the members purchased every bottle of champagne left in the club so that we could enjoy some bucks fizz. I joined them for a half hour and left them finishing off the rest of the champagne.

Four years later the 1987 General Election was a disaster for the Conservative Party in Scotland. We lost eleven Parliamentary seats, and were left with only nine MPs north of the Border.

My share of the vote fell to 39.48 per cent but this still gave me a 6,014 majority over Ralph Leishman, the SDP/Alliance candidate (now a Conservative), and I was content with the fact that despite the difficult times the Party was facing in Scotland, 19,388 voters had put their cross against my name. After that election the Eastwood Conservative Association published *Apostles not Apologists*, a pamphlet arguing that Scottish Tories must stick to our principles in both national and local policies.

The 1987 General Election was the third in which Margaret Thatcher had led the Conservative Party to victory but it was also to be her last. I have described my view of the events surrounding her departure elsewhere in this book but I would like to state here my admiration for Margaret both as a politician and as a person.

In the run up to the 1992 General Election the media was not only writing off the Party's chances of forming a Government after April 9, but also predicting a possible wipe-out of Tory MPs in Scotland.

Both predictions proved to be well wide of the mark. John Major took the election by the scruff of the neck and won over the voters. In Scotland, far from being wiped out, we increased our share of the vote and we won back Kincardine and Deeside from the Liberal Democrats and took Aberdeen South from Labour.

I had never believed the doom and gloom merchants. The story I was getting on the ground in my own constituency was that I would once again receive the backing of the Eastwood electorate. John Major had made opposition to devolution a prime platform in his campaign across the United Kingdom and my views on this subject were well known throughout the constituency and I had no fears on this question.

In addition there were two local issues which we campaigned on. Those were the completion of the M77 which would ease the transport problems of a lot of constituents and also the Keep Eastwood Out of Glasgow campaign, which Conservatives had been fighting to support ever since the District was born. It was a campaign which drew a great deal of popular support.

The Liberal Democrats who as the SDP/Alliance had come second in the last two General Elections were claiming that 1992 was to be their year. Their candidate, Moira Craig was prominent in the Scottish Constitutional Convention and was a vice convener of the Campaign for a Scottish Assembly. Labour's candidate was Peter Grant-Hutchison, an advocate, while the SNP put up Paul Scott. I should not forget that the Natural Law Party also had a candidate, Lee Ferguson, but he was not very active in the campaign as he was working as a lecturer in the United States.

The result was tremendous fillip to our local party workers. The Conservative vote shot up from 19,388 to 24,124 while Labour came in second with 12,436 votes.

My success as Member of Parliament for Eastwood since 1979 has of course been due in large measure to the support and immense hard work of the constituency association chairmen, their office bearers and staff – Jim Goold, Peter Edmondson, Adrian Shinwell, Jackson Carlaw, Cliff Hargreaves, Ian Muir are but a few of the chairmen who have ably and voluntarily shouldered the considerable burden of work over the period. We have also had excellent councillors at Strathclyde Region, in Renfrew District and in Eastwood, where Provost Leslie Rosin and his colleagues recently took a number of excellent initiatives in the arts and twinning which will be continued into the new authority.

## CHAPTER 12

# FOUR SECRETARIES OF STATE

Being Secretary of State for Scotland is not for the fainthearted or thin-skinned. Like it or not, you are also the Cabinet's man in Scotland. To some extent the Secretary of State is at the mercy of events. If any problem, real or perceived, arises the inevitable cry goes up for the Secretary of State to 'do something'. All official Scottish Office decisions are taken in the Secretary of State's office. In practice some are taken by Junior Ministers, many minor ones (notably on planning) by officials acting under delegated powers.

There are some oddities about the decision making process, especially on planning decisions. The Secretary of State or the Planning Minister may profoundly disagree with an appeal decision taken under delegated powers. There is nothing they can do except in theory change the legislation. The decision goes out in the Secretary of State's name and ordinary people, not versed in the intricacies of bureaucratic practice, naturally assume the Secretary of State took the decision himself.

Identifiable public expenditure is relatively high in Scotland. One might believe this would result in the demand for more public spending being lower than south of the border. In practice the reverse is true. High levels of spending mean high numbers of beneficiaries of the taxpayers' largesse. They all want more, not necessarily for themselves personally but for the cause or group they represent. The general interest of the taxpayers is in keeping public expenditure down, but that interest is disparate and not usually organised. The pressure groups are all persuasive, often worthy and usually express their just demands as being manifestly in the public interest. The same system of course confronted Labour Secretaries of State for Scotland prior to 1979.

The subsequent Conservative Secretaries of State faced additional difficulties. They had to deal with major industrial closures – Ravenscraig, Linwood, Bathgate, and Invergordon. Ironically all these industrial giants were located in Scotland because previous Conservative Governments, with the best of intentions, had interfered with the normal operation of market forces. With the wisdom of hindsight, it is easy to say how they should never have been there in the first place, although the respective industrial stories are more complicated than that. What is certainly true is that such closures made life politically very difficult for the Secretaries of State involved.

Also, and in marked contrast to their Labour predecessors, the four Conservative Secretaries of State have had the support of only a minority of Scottish MPs. In one sense that has not been of crucial importance. Malcolm Rifkind famously referred to his 'Gatling Gun' – that in a United Kingdom Parliament, the overall majority would eventually prevail, assuring no rebellions among the Government's supporters. But politics is not that simple. It consists not just of the House of Commons votes but of trying to influence positively the electorate and in Scotland the largely home grown political system. In practice non MPs in Scotland have had to play an unusually high role – Party Chairmen and leading office bearers such as Lord Goold, Sir Michael Hirst, John Mackay, Annabel Goldie, Jackson Carlaw, Adrian Shinwell, Russel Sanderson and Bill Hughes have had a much higher profile and a great deal more media work than would have been the case if more Scottish Tory MPs had been elected to support the four Scottish Secretaries.

The facts are well known and need to be only briefly recapitulated. Prime Minister James Callaghan, having inexplicably not gone to the country in 1978, was brought down by the Winter of Discontent and the devolution issue. In 1979 a revitalised Scottish Tory Party under Teddy Taylor gained seven seats from the SNP – the 'turkeys voting for an early Christmas'. The European elections in 1979 returned five Scottish Tories to two Labour MEPs and Winnie Ewing for the SNP in the Highlands and Islands. Despite the disaster of losing Teddy Taylor in Cathcart, the incoming administration had a solid base of Scottish parliamentary support. In 1983, Margaret Thatcher swept home to a post-Falklands War landslide, much assisted by a Labour campaign of quite startling ineptitude. But the overall position in Scotland was slightly weakened. In 1983 George Younger, then Malcolm Rifkind had a Scottish Tory team of 21 out of 72 MPs. Redistribution made analysis rather complicated but it would not be reasonable to regard that result as an overall net loss of one compared to 1979. Hamish Gray's loss of Ross, Cromarty and Skye as the SDP and Liberal Democrats swept the Highlands and the failure to regain Glasgow Hillhead from Roy Jenkins was not wholly compensated for by Anna McCurley's famous victory in Renfrew West and Inverclyde, a win undoubtedly in considerable measure due to Anna's indomitable will and bubbling personality.

In 1987 Magaret Thatcher went safely on to her third term. Essex man (and woman) among others stood firm. In Scotland six seats were lost to Labour, three to the SNP and two to the Liberal Democrats. It was a disaster with which Malcolm Rifkind had to contend and did so brilliantly. Politics is not only about numbers.

It is about perception. It might on the force of it seem that way with Ian Lang's position after 1992.

In practice that is not the way politics works. Eleven may not seem very different from ten, but when nearly every political pundit has been forecasting a wipeout and you have more supporters after the battle than before, the landscape looks suddenly different. Nevertheless to a different degree all four Secretaries of State faced the same problem of minority support.

Much is made of the discretion Secretaries of State for Scotland have over how to allocate the very substantial sums of taxpayers' money they control. In reality I suspect all four found themselves much more constrained than the rhetoric suggests. Total expenditure within the Secretary of State's responsibility in the current year (1996/7) is over £14.5 billion, which sounds and is a great deal of money. Technically the Scottish Secretary of State has complete discretion over the 95% of that which comes under the 'Scottish block'. Expenditure outside the block is agriculture, fisheries and food and finance for nationalised industries.

The key factor which determines the size of the Scottish block is variously known as the 'Goschen-Barnett Formula' or the 'Barnett Rules', after Joel, now Lord, Barnett, Labour's Chief Secretary to the Treasury in 1978 when the formula was introduced in preparation for the financing of a Scottish Assembly. *Scotland In The Union: A Partnership For Good* includes perhaps the clearest definition of the Barnett Rules (paras 2.13, 2.14):

> The Secretary of State's spending programmes fall into two main categories: those within the Scottish Block and those outside it. The programmes outside the block are mainly those where there is a requirement for a standard policy across Great Britain or the United Kingdom. Planned spending outside the block is settled by separate negotiation.
>
> For the programmes within the block, a different procedure applies under the rules which apply to territorial departments, Scotland (like Wales and Northern Ireland) automatically takes a proportion of changes to expenditure plans in the annual

public expenditure survey for comparable expenditure by
territorial or Whitehall departments. That proportion is
calculated by reference to a population related formula which
was updated in the 1992 Public Expenditure Survey, to take
into account the results of the 1991 census, so that it is now
10.66% of spending changes in England. The Secretary of State's
block programmes emerged from the 1992 Survey with
spending in Scotland over 30% higher on a per capita basis than
spending on comparable services in England.

So far so good. If £100 million is added to planned National Health
Service expenditure in England then £10.66 million is added to the
Scottish block which Ministers may or may not add to NHS
spending in Scotland.

But life for the Secretary of State is not quite that simple. There
may be in a year expenditure adjustments not subject to the
formula, special circumstances of one form or another, and
changes of responsibility between the Scottish Office and
Whitehall departments – such as the transfer of training and higher
education to the Scottish Office in recent years. In particular the
figures for equivalent English expenditure are often difficult to
establish.

In the real political world our Secretary of State would not
find it easy to reallocate the £10.66 million in the example above,
to say, the roads programme. The Health Minister and all his
officials will point out the practical and political problems. How
could such an obviously different policy be justified. In addition,
most programmes are ongoing. In any given year there are heavy
inherited commitments – notably wages and salaries for public
sector staff.

So our four Secretaries of State have all faced political,
economic and public expenditure constraints. How have they
reacted? These thoughts do not in any way aspire to be a
comprehensive account of their respective tenures of office. Rather
they are personal snapshots of the four men who have been
responsible for guiding Scotland's affairs since 1979.

Many commentators have discussed the relationship

between Ministers and Civil Servants. The Scottish Office in terms of numbers is an extremely large Government Department – as has often been pointed out, at times larger than the European Commission (depending on definitions).

In my experience, the relations between Secretaries of State and the Civil Service varied in personnel terms but seldom in effectiveness. The two Permanent Under Secretaries of State over the period, Sir William Kerr Fraser and Sir Russell Hillhouse are highly intelligent and politically sophisticated. Certainly when I was a very new Junior Minister I often relied considerably for sage advice on the vastly experienced Kerr Fraser.

The key to an effective relationship between Ministers and the Civil Service is the performance of Ministerial Private Offices, the staff of which report to the Secretary of State's Private Secretary. So that appointment (the Secretary of State's own) becomes absolutely critical to how the whole machine performs. It is perhaps invidious to name Civil Servants still pursuing their own careers.

### George Younger

George Younger had not expected to be Secretary of State. But he started with several advantages. He had a strong Ministerial team and a group of enthusiastic backbenchers. It is interesting that of that group, Michael Ancram, Gerry Malone, Iain Sproat, John Mackay and Peter Fraser are all Ministers of State in the present Government although none sits for a Scottish seat. That attests to both durability and personal ability.

George Younger came with a wealth of personal experience. He had been a Scottish Office Minister and Minister of State for Defence under Ted Heath. Earlier his 'Save The Argylls' campaign had made him a household name throughout Scotland. He had particularly endeared himself to the Conservative Party by resigning the nomination for Kinross and West Perthshire to Sir Alec Douglas Home to give the then Prime Minister a route back into the Commons.

Working with him, perhaps the main characteristic that

struck me was how calm he always remained however many difficulties had to be faced. It is believed George Younger lost his temper only once at the Scottish Office – when his Private Secretary went off in his official car, leaving the Secretary of State stranded. His imperturbability was legendary. Relations with local government were always somewhat fraught, but meetings were usually courteous. At one time however, a COSLA delegate launched a personal attack on George, accusing him among other things of being the worst Secretary of State Scotland had ever experienced. There was a horrified silence. The Secretary of State commented with a slight smile, "Have you tried one of the chocolate biscuits?" End of crisis.

George and his Industry Minister, the late Sir Alex Fletcher, had to deal with a whole series of major industrial crises. I was heavily involved in the first, the Linwood car plant, since the factory (not the town of Linwood) was then in East Renfrewshire. I knew when the end came. It was when George Younger asked the owners, "What would it cost to keep Linwood open?" and they replied, "a guarantee from the Government to buy all the cars."

George Younger's charm and calm often deceived people into believing he lacked determination. Not true. Whether or not he did threaten to resign in 1982 over Ravenscraig I do not know. But he certainly worked unceasingly in its defence.

While the industrial crises inherited from the past dominated the headlines, the Scottish economy was being steadily restructured. The formation of Locate in Scotland was a master stroke which improved our cutting edge in the hard competitive world of inward investment. Scotland's relative position in the UK improved consistently. On some occasions George Younger would take a strong market line. For example on allowing competition on the London Scottish air routes (introduced by Iain Sproat), although for constituency reasons he supported the maintenance of the Prestwick Airport transatlantic monopoly – as did the overwhelming majority of Scottish MPs.

The continuing problems with the high levels of local authority spending came to a real crisis with the rates revaluation in the spring of 1985. Not only did the revaluation switch the rates burden sharply on to the domestic ratepayer, the rate support grant settlement was tight and its distribution singularly unhelpful to councils such as Eastwood District. The result was the biggest crisis of George Younger's period in office and the end of the domestic rating system.

The history of the Community Charge or Poll Tax has been well documented. But there is one major misperception. The Poll Tax was introduced a year ahead in Scotland. It is believed this was because the English wanted to try the idea out in Scotland – that we Scots were being used as some kind of laboratory experiment. The reverse is the case. It was the Scottish Office Ministers and the Scottish Conservative Party who persuaded the Government to move quickly in Scotland. There was no pressure to do so from the Treasury or the Department of the Environment, which consistantly opposed having revaluations in England – illogical but politically sensible.

The relationship between Secretaries of State and Junior Ministers varies greatly. Harold Wilson used to balance his Ministries with representatives from different wings of the Labour Party – hardly a recipe for departmental harmony. Ministers are appointed by the Prime Minister. But their remits are determined by the Secretary of State and so is their scope for independent action.

George Younger let his Junior Ministers get on with things while he concentrated on the major issues. Ministers reviewed issues of concern regularly every Wednesday morning and as necessary. George trusted the judgement of his team.

It was no surprise when he was promoted to Defence when Michael Heseltine resigned in January 1986 following the Westland crisis. What was a surprise was his resignation in 1989 when he also announced he was not standing for Parliament again in order to become Chairman of the Royal Bank of Scotland. He achieved a great deal for Scotland, ran a happy team and undoubtedly his personality defused a great deal of hostility in times of difficulty.

*Allan Stewart at the age of eleven*
*while at Castlehill Primary School, Cupar*

*a young student at St Andrews University*

*Allan and his wife Susie in the garden of their home in Neilston*

*Allan Stewart with Mrs Thatcher at a Conservative Party function the morning after she had announced that she was not standing for re-election as Party Leader*

*Col Gadaffi, the President of Libya, greets Allan Stewart at the entrance to his tent during a visit to Libya in April 1995*

*a family portrait of Allan Stewart with his wife Susie and children,*
*son Garath and daughter Rosa*

*Allan Stewart chats with Prime Minister John Major and Roman Catholic Bishop Mone of Paisley at the February 1994 Focus on Scotland dinner in the Hilton Hotel, Glasgow*

*The new Scottish Office team following the 1992 General Election.*
*Scottish Secretary of State Ian Lang flanked left to right by*
*Minister of State Lord Fraser of Carmylie;*
*Lord James Douglas-Hamilton, education and housing;*
*Allan Stewart, industry and local government;*
*and Sir Hector Munro, agriculture and the environment*

## Malcolm Rifkind

When I was a colleague of Malcom Rifkind's back in 1981, a parliamentary colleague asked me my opinion of him. I said I thought he would eventually become Foreign Secretary or Secretary of State for Scotland. As events have turned out, this forecast was correct on both counts.

It is well-known I declined when asked to return to the Scottish Office after the 1987 General Election. Some have interpreted this as suggesting some kind of personal difference with Malcolm Rifkind. That is simply not true. After my experience as Education Minister, I had determined never to take up ministerial office again. I wanted to be a backbencher – the Honourable Member for Eastwood.

Malcolm Rifkind is a brilliant debater. The country does not now have the chance to hear and see Malcolm winding up a debate. (Foreign Secretaries do not wind up debates in the House of Commons, except possibly a debate opened by the Prime Minister.) When he did, he performed the function better than anyone else I have heard. It is much easier to open a debate for the Government than wind one up. The opening speech is well prepared beforehand and there is some flexibility about its length. The best wind up speech is one which actually answers the debate. It should refer to as many of the points made by Members as possible but should be coherent and above all it must stop exactly on time – between 9.59 and 10pm for major debates. Not an easy task! Sitting down is of course easy enough in itself but sitting down after concluding with a well-argued presentation is difficult. Doing it with few if any notes is brilliant. Doing that consistently is unique. Malcolm has the advocate's ability to master a brief in a remarkably short time.

The sharpness of his intellect was brought forcibly home in the first 'Public Expenditure Survey' discussions in which I participated (October 1981). Having worked with these matters before, I was under the slight misapprehension that I understood what PES was all about. Malcolm was absolutely dazzling on behalf of his Department. The huge health budget for which I was responsible soon came under pressure. However, one learns. During a break I was asked to identify savings – not cuts since the total health budget was as usual expanding. I returned and was able to announce that by postponing certain projects savings could be made. George Younger and Malcolm both looked extremely pleased, until the list was read out. By one of those strange coincidences projects in Ayr and Edinburgh figured highly in the list. Further negotiation proved necessary.

Much has been made of Malcolm Rifkind's early support for devolution. But he always made it clear he envisaged a coherent scheme which included England. It was Malcolm who coined the phrase 'unilateral devolution' which goes to the heart of the weakness of Labour's proposals.

Malcolm's greatest achievement as a Junior Minister in the Scottish Office was to put through the legislation which gave Scottish council tenants the right to buy their own homes. This has transformed the economic position of hundreds of thousands of families and literally changed the face of Scotland as driving through housing estates now amply confirms.

As Secretary of State he introduced Scottish Enterprise, Highlands and Islands Enterprise and the system of business led local enterprise companies and he privatised the Scottish Bus Group. Some of the smaller actions he took were very important for particular areas of interest – for example finding some £8 million to finance a huge expansion of Gaelic broadcasting.

What of the great row over the Law Reform (Miscellaneous Provisions) Bill in the early summer of 1990 and the chairmanship of Michael Forsyth? The publicity was generated by three factors. First when the row over the Bill blew up, nothing much else was on the political landscape. This previously little known Bill, which Peter Fraser had very successfully steered through the Lords, was the only show in town. Second, an implacable opponent was Nicky Fairbairn with whom Malcolm had had a blazing row. The row was private but needless to say very much public within about twenty minutes. Third, alleged supporters of Malcolm and Michael, probably without their knowledge or consent, were hyping everything up in the press.

That Bill was not Malcolm's creation, nor that of Lord James. But it was in reality some five Bills, to which the civil servants kept adding further and generally daft ideas – such as not allowing churches with a membership below a certain figure full charitable status (as I pointed out to colleagues – lo, the Scottish Office would have defined Our Lord and the Twelve Apostles as a second class church). That particular proposal collapsed when I asked whether the Jewish and Muslim churches had been consulted. They had not.

It was a classic Civil Service Bill. The executive was trying to pull several fast ones over the legislature on a Bill which had not been foreseen in the governing party's election manifesto. They tried to get the committee to go right through one Thursday night – wholly without precedent for Scottish Members. Fortunately for me the subject of the accounts of charities came up and I had taken the precaution of obtaining every known authoritative article on the subject. With considerable help from Nicky, Bill Walker and Donald Dewar's team on the other side, I made it clear I could speak for at least four hours without any difficulty. Malcolm ordered that the proceedings should be finished at a reasonable hour. When he was subsequently convinced that I was not part of any plot, did not in principle oppose the Bill but felt we could not sensibly pass so much legislative detail in the time reasonably available, Malcolm acted brilliantly. He produced a package which he discussed with interested parties, notably the Law Society of Scotland and the MPs most directly concerned. The interview I had with Malcolm was probably the shortest of the series. He outlined his proposals. I told him he had met my concerns and his proposaals had my unequivocal support which I would express both publicly and privately.

The reputed conflict with Michael Forsyth (then Scottish Party Chairman) was obviously a difficult period throughout 1990. I would describe myself as an involved non-participant. Some of the press reports appeared to me quite extraordinary.

In retrospect, Malcolm's position was difficult. He had an

able, highly motivated, Junior Minister with the personal ear of the Prime Minister, who had appointed him Scottish Party Chairman. With the wisdom of hindsight the idea of having a Junior Scottish Office Minister as Party Chairman was almost certainly a mistake. It has not been repeated, because of the clear potential for conflict.

Scottish business has a particular reason for gratitude to Malcolm, and Ian Lang, his then Industry Minister. In 1989 he made the commitment to bring Scottish business rates into line with those in England and Wales. The importance of that policy has been generally under-estimated. Yet it has underpinned the success of the Scottish economy (at great financial cost) throughout the 1990s.

Baroness Thatcher has in her memoirs criticised Malcolm's tenure at the Scottish Office as not being sufficiently Thatcherite. However, in my view Malcolm was not then, and is not now, a wet. He may have obtained such a reputation because of his traditional interest in devolution (not in principle a wet/dry issue) and in a range of social policies. He is a natural debater and often argues purely for the fun of exchanging ideas.

### Ian Lang

I knew Ian Lang quite well before he joined the Scottish Office team and went on to become Secretary of State for Scotland. He had been a member of the Party for a long time and he first stood for election to Parliament at the same time as I did. When he stood in June 1970 for Central Ayrshire I was pounding the campaign trail in Dundee East.

We eventually entered Parliament at the same time following the 1979 General Election, although Ian had fought the Pollok seat in February 1974 when James White won it for Labour. Our parallel career paths continued when we both made our Maiden Speeches on the same day.

Ian and I became more closely involved with each other when he became my whip between 1981 and 1986, and although I was a Scottish Office Minister and whips are more involved with backbenchers, Ian would still keep me informed about Parliamentary business. He was very competent and was always aware of what was happening in the House.

Ian's first ministerial experience came at the Department of Employment where he was appointed an Under Secretary of State in 1986 before he moved later that year to the Scottish Office again as an Under Secretary of State following my resignation.

He became Secretary of State for Scotland in 1990 and I joined his team. I took over the responsibilities he had held before John Major promoted him, although not as a Minister of State. Ian continued to take a great interest in the areas which were now my responsibility but I found that we instinctively agreed on most matters. Ian did not devolve in the way that George Younger did. He took a great deal of interest in the detailed working of departments and we held more meetings than we did under George.

In Parliament Ian was always very cool, as he showed in his recent handling of the Scott Report.

Following the Kincardine byelection defeat Ian called a meeting in Dover House of the Scottish Office ministers. Present at the meeting were Michael Forsyth, Lord Strathclyde, Lord James and myself. It was a private meeting without the attendance of civil servants as we were discussing political matters. At this meeting we all agreed that we should stick firmly by our principled stand against devolution. It was agreed that we would uphold the Union and not muddy the waters.

Following this meeting Ian went to John Major and this is when it was decided to make the Union a major plank in our General Election campaign right across the United Kingdom.

I would not rule out Ian Lang being a candidate in the future for Leader of the Party and Prime Minister. He is now much better known in England in his present position as President of the Board of Trade.

**Michael Forsyth**

Although I have not served under Michael Forsyth in his capacity as Secretary of State for Scotland we have worked together as Ministers and we are personal friends.

Our paths never crossed at St Andrews University where Michael was President of the Conservative Association from 1972–75 but I certainly knew of him as he was a tremendous pamphleteer, producing a wide range of papers. He of course is on the same political wavelength as myself believing in free markets, and is a founder member of the No Turning Back Group. Our paths first met when I met him at functions during his spell as chairman of the Federation of Conservative Students.

Michael arrived in Parliament following the 1983 General Election when he won the Stirling seat and he was very supportive during the EIS dispute as he disagreed strongly with the Union's tactic of targetting constituencies.

I describe Michael as the Stirling Streetfighter. He is politically very active and like Margaret Thatcher he enjoys a good political argument. His style attracted a great deal of attention during the period he was chairman of the Party in Scotland in 1989 and 1990. It was a period when Malcolm Rifkind was Secretary of State and John Mackay was chief executive of the Party. All three were highly political animals. Normally the chief executive position is not a very political one, and no one has suggested since that we should have a junior minister who is also Party chairman.

However my impression is that because there was a great deal of media comment concerning rows between them that any conflict was built up by so-called supporters rather than by Malcolm, John and Michael. It was supposed to be over the soul of the Party but personally I do not believe that. It was blown out of all proportion. Certainly Michael was trying to do a lot very quickly but that is his style. He looks for opportunities and works very hard to achieve success.

In Parliament he is an excellent tactician. During the 1987–88 session the School Boards Bill was going through and there was the row over Paisley Grammar which Strathclyde Region wanted to close. Michael was responsible for the Bill's progress through Parliament and he and Malcolm changed the regulations so that the Region could not close the school.

The Opposition was mounting a highly vocal campaign against the Bill but Michael drafted in English backbenchers who were members of the No Turning Back Group on to the Committee, and we would meet half an hour before the committee to discuss tactics.

Normally backbenchers are not involved by Ministers but Michael would bring us all right up to date with what was happening, and encouraged us to intervene. This meant that instead of a series of critical questions which would be reported by the media we had Government backbenchers making clever interventions, such as Edward Leigh and Michael Brown, and this had to be reflected by the reporters covering the meetings.

Michael has benefited from his experience as a Minister of State for two UK departments and while he is perceived to be more mellow, he remains a fanatical worker. He will always take the battle to the Opposition and has a remarkable talent for 'one-liners' and soundbites. His invention of the terms 'roof tax' and now 'tartan tax' both transformed political debate in Scotland. Most politicians use a hundred words when ten will do. Michael uses two. Further he has united the Party – for example by bringing in to the centre of things, Brian Meek and Arthur Bell. Personally his energy and sharpness remind one above all of Michael Heseltine.

## CHAPTER 13

# TWO PRIME MINISTERS

Perhaps inevitably acres of newspaper columns and books have compared the qualities, personalities and records of Margaret Thatcher and John Major. One gets the impression that if one winter morning Margaret remarked, "It's snowing hard," some bright spark would interpret that as a call for a review of cold weather payments. It is extraordinarily difficult for the new Baroness Thatcher to say anything in public without it being analysed endlessly for any possible implied criticism of the Prime Minister. From John Major's point of view the questions about whether he is a true heir of the Thatcher legacy still go on – more than four years after he obtained his own mandate in the 1992 General Election.

I have served as a Minister and backbencher under both – an unusual perspective. I voted for both in leadership contests.

Margaret Thatcher, as a historical footnote, has an interesting connection with the Eastwood constituency. Betty Harvie Anderson, my predecessor, was a close friend of Margaret. At one time they shared a House Of Commons office and Betty was one of Margaret's key supporters when she ran for the party leadership against Ted Heath. After she won, her first political engagement was to speak in Betty's constituency – in Clarkston. After Margaret made her irrevocable announcement not to stand again for the Commons – so giving up any chance of a return as Conservative Leader – her first engagement was a coffee morning in Eastwood. She gave of course a typically brilliant, barnstorming performance, bashing Brussels and much of its centralist works around the proverbial park.

When the 1974 election defeats meant Ted Heath was up for re-election, I was a member of the executive of the Beckenham Conservative Association. Just before the final list of candidates was announced, the MP Philip Goodheart asked the executive to vote for their preferred candidate. A fairly large number had been publicly rumoured as possible. Ted Heath came top of that particular ballot, with Willie Whitelaw second. Margaret Thatcher received one clear vote – mine.

That demonstrates one similarity between Margaret Thatcher and John Major. Neither were particularly well known to the broader public when they became party leader. They were however very well known in the Parliamentary Conservative Party.

I have discussed the election which brought Margaret Thatcher to the leadership with a number of those involved, including Norman Tebbit, one of Margaret Thatcher's key campaign organisers. First of all, there is no doubt that she had a well-organised campaign. Second, market oriented MPs, appalled by Ted Heath's prices and incomes policy, were gunning for him. But third, she had been personally charming and helpful to a large number of backbench MPs. Ted Heath was and is a person of formidable intellect and determination. But suffering gladly those he regards as fools is not perhaps his leading personal characteristic.

Similarly John Major had met and impressed a large number of his colleagues during his steady rise up through the Ministerial ranks. I recall when he was Chief Secretary being one of a group of backbenchers discussing our pet proposals for the forthcoming Budget. He had no idea what anyone was going to raise. Yet his grasp of general problems and technical detail was immense. It startled some of those MPs who did not know him well.

Another common characteristic of the two Prime Ministers is their background – dissimilar in many respects but common in being not of the traditional ranks from which the Tory leadership has been drawn. Both have both been very fortunate in their spouses. People involved in party politics are just like anyone else. The demands on a Prime Minister's time are enormous. Many party functions, although they have a political purpose are essentially social. So a husband or wife can be a completely acceptable stand-in – so long as they do not offend people. Sir Dennis Thatcher and Norma Major have both received – deservedly – a generally favourable press. Both are extremely popular and hard working. Such good qualities are not just personally and socially desirable. They are politically important too.

The popular perception is that John Major is a much less determined personality than Margaret Thatcher. No one can doubt the determination of the Iron Lady. "This Lady's not for turning," was one of her most memorable and accurate lines. But the popular view is so often over-simplified as to end up being positively inaccurate. John Major is patently determined. No one entering Parliament in 1979 and becoming Prime Minister in 1990 could possibly be otherwise.

In my experience Margaret Thatcher had an enormous asset in Willie Whitelaw. It was not for nothing she told a Party Conference " every woman needs a Willie", a line which resulted in inexplicable mirth from some of the less respectful elements.

Willie Whitelaw's career was motivated throughout by an absolute sense of loyalty. His importance to Margaret was not only that unimpeachable quality however. Willie's judgement and integrity were wholly trusted by more traditional sections of the Conservative Party which tended often to suspect Margaret Thatcher's radical reforming zeal. The old guard and the 'Knights of the Shires' relied on Willie. Willie always knew everything that was going on.

Margaret Thatcher cared a great deal about Scotland and was puzzled by Scots' opposition to the Conservative and Unionist Party. She worked enormously hard on her Scottish visits and speeches. Before one of her Scottish Conference speeches, I happened to be the Scottish Office Duty Minister so was asked to No. 10 to help prepare it. After a morning session a small group of advisers and myself met at about 5.30pm. I left at 11pm to catch the sleeper. I felt both exhilarated and drained. Hour after hour the Prime Minister had poured her apparently inexhaustible sources of energy into the work – asking questions, throwing out comments, weighing the merits of different ways of saying much the same thing. It was immensely impressive. So of course was the speech when she came to deliver it. Legend has it Margaret Thatcher needs only 3–4 hours sleep at night. I can well believe it.

Margaret Thatcher as Prime Minister greatly liked argument. Often this was simply to test the strength of a proposition being put to her. Often it was for the sake of it. Because of pressure of work Ministers often become less concerned with ideas as time goes on. That was never true of Margaret.

She rewarded loyalty with loyalty. During the bitter coal strike, led by Arthur Scargill, the steel workers at Ravenscraig insisted on continuing to work. Questions were raised about the desirability of allowing ore imports into Hunterston to be transported by lorry to Ravenscraig despite heavy picketing. The Prime Minister absolutely insisted we had to do everything possible to ensure the supplies went in.

As Prime Minister, Margaret Thatcher certainly seemed to be blamed personally in Scotland for every problem and every grievance, however imagined or slight.

A constituent told me of an incident which highlighted that climate of opinion. She was having a new window fitted to her council flat. The frame did not fit. Her enquiries were met with a furious tirade about 'the cuts' and an assurance that "it's all the fault of that bloody woman".

My constituent paused then commented, "I know what Margaret Thatcher would say if she were here."

"What's that?"

"She'd say turn that frame round. You're trying to put it in the wrong way up!" The frame was correctly inserted, during a period of silence.

As one who argued to the bitter end that Margaret Thatcher should contest the second ballot during the last leadership election I would certainly have known if John Major took part, directly or indirectly, in any plot against the Prime Minister. The answer is an unequivocal no. At no point did those former Margaret Thatcher allies use his name in advocating she stand down.

What happened was really very simple. After the first ballot Margaret Thatcher was just two votes short of the necessary majority. She was however in Paris. The Michael Heseltine supporters were clearly on a roll and picking up pledges of support for the second ballot. Basically a large section of the Parliamentary members panicked, including many leading Ministers. Westminster is often described as a hothouse. This was a hothouse with the thermostat at fever pitch.

Margaret Thatcher will go down in history as one of the great Prime Ministers on a par with Pitt and Churchill. She changed things irreversibly. The main difference between the two Premierships is that the challenges facing Margaret Thatcher were much clearer than those facing John Major. For example the curbing of trade union power; giving the unions back to the members; standing up to Arthur Scargill; and the Falklands War. These issues were all very clear and Margaret Thatcher was well equipped to deal with them.

Today the issues facing us and John Major are much more

shaded, less black and white. John Major's strength is his ability to listen and his preparedness to indulge in patient arguments and work matters through over a period of time. The manner in which he has handled Northern Ireland is a good example of his strengths. No one knows how the present initiative is going to turn out, but one thing is certain – a lot of people are alive today who would have been dead if John Major had not pursued his peace initiative.

The truth is that most people exaggerate the difference between them. Margaret Thatcher was actually more pragmatic than people appreciate. She was also more cautious than her public image suggested. Margaret of course developed her 'the lady is not for turning' image which served Britain very well particularly abroad.

John Major's two strengths are that he is good when dealing with individuals as was shown when he got on the soapbox during the last General Election campaign. Many so-called political pundits decried this but it appealed to the ordinary person in the streets. He also has great patience and a grasp of detail. I witnessed this at first hand during our meetings concerning help for Lanarkshire. We had several meetings on our own at 10 Downing Street and he was concerned the area could go into downward spiral if we did not focus on the future and put in additional resources.

His strengths are suited for the complex times we live in while Margaret Thatcher was ideal for the clear challenges of the 1980s.

CHAPTER 14

# ALLIES AND OPPONENTS

**Donald Dewar**

Commentators and many MPs were surprised when Donald Dewar emerged as Opposition Chief Whip. Senior whips (on both sides) are traditionally seen as silent hard men. Donald did not appear to fit in with either adjective.

The point about silence was soon met. There are good reasons for whips' traditional silence on general party matters. Whips are members of a Government (or Opposition) front bench but have no specific policy responsibilities. That is the task of others, so if whips start talking about policy there is a clear risk of conflict and confusion. The task of the whips, putting it at its simplest, is to keep the show on the road.

Yet Donald Dewar's speaking role has been a success and by common consent he is doing an excellent job as Labour's Chief Whip. My own view is that either by good luck or by good judgement Tony Blair realised a key point about Donald Dewar, that he is a man for government.

Opposition Chief Whip is a real job, rightly paid. If an Opposition Chief Whip cannot do his job, his party suffers. But it is more than a party job. If relations between the Opposition whips and the Government break down, all hell breaks loose. MPs (as has happened) can find themselves in the House of Commons in Committee staying up all night for no good purpose. That does nobody any benefit, least of all the institution of Parliament, since the electorate not unnaturally concludes we must be off our collective trolleys. So the job of Opposition Chief Whip matters.

Donald Dewar is in politics to do a front line but a real, detailed, hard job. That is not the motivation of every Member of Parliament, other than in relation to their own constituents. Many are there simply to be backbenchers or because of particular ideas or principles they wish to advocate.

Just as well, really. If everyone wanted to be a Prime Minister the House of Commons would be impossible.

Allied to a wish to do things as well as talk about them is Donald's sense of fairness. This is widely recognised by political allies and opponents alike. (Donald appears to have no enemies, or if there are, they do not admit it).

This was brought home to me when we first met after I came to my CBI job in Glasgow. Just about my first media engagemnent was to do an interview with Donald who then hosted a political programmme on Radio Clyde. In 1976 Radio Clyde was in the depths of Glasgow's Anderston Cross Centre – well before its present efficient splendour in Clydebank.

Cutting a long story short, I was terribly late. Donald would have been entirely justified in saying so, thus landing me in hot water with CBI members who rightly would have taken the view that the salary they paid involved spokesmen getting to interviews on time. Donald skilfully filled in the time, gave me two minutes

144

to regain my breath and moved smoothly into the interview.

Then when the Scottish Affairs Select Committee was set up in 1981, Donald was the first Chairman. That itself was controversial since the Committee (like all Select Committees) had a Government majority. On our first report, the organisation of inward investment, the Committee split on party lines, with the Conservatives amending Donald's Report. There was a tremendous furore.

I watched and listened to Donald on a number of interviews. Again and again he was invited by interviewers who had patently not read the Report to attack the Conservative members. Again and again he explained patiently and fairly that we believed this, he understood for these reasons, whereas he and his colleagues believed the best structure would be something different. In the event, of course, George Younger resolved the problem by creating what no one had thought of – Locate In Scotland.

The point is that most politicians in Donald's position would simply have put the boot in. But what Edward Pearce in the *Daily Telegraph* has called Donald's "endearing attachment to rectitude" ruled supreme.

I would not dream of describing Donald Dewar as a Blairite. First the term is meaningless and second Donald Dewar was an influential figure in Scotland when Tony Blair was charging around the playground at Fettes College. It is always dangerous to label politicians but Donald Dewar seems in the Gaitskellite tradition, if that is said still to exist.

One final political point about Donald. In my Ministerial experience, Scottish MPs, irrespective of party, work extremely hard for their constituents. But Donald's letters were different. He always wrote a covering letter, analysing his constituent's problem, the pros and cons, the legislation that was relevant, points that the constituent might have missed.

Any Member of Parliament worth his or hers salt collects stories that go into the Westminster legends. Usually there is a least an element of truth in the story. The story is that Donald received an agitated call from the police. His House of Commons room had been burgled. Could he come at once ? He did.

The room had been locked.The police threw the door open. Papers everywhere, files upturned, filing cabinets opened. The place was in a shambles. It is reputed that Donald reviewed the scene, shuffled a bit, then told the anxious constabulary, "Sorry, officers, it usually looks like this." Donald Dewar is not known for office tidiness nor personal ambition. But for meticulous work, fairness, commitment to his own beliefs, he has, as they say, the respect of the House.

## Robin Cook

Scotland is a small and intense political world. Glasgow is a very short distance from Edinburgh, as is St Andrews and Dundee. But I have to admit that I had not really come across Robin Cook before we met in the House Of Commons.

The only reason therefore that I include him in these short sketches is a simple one – in my view he is the Labour spokesman the Tories should most fear. The last person that was really said of was Denis (now Lord) Healey whom, to the astonished relief of the entire Conservative Party, Labour did not elect as Leader.

I had not come across Robin Cook before entering Parliament in 1979, except by reputation. After contesting against Alex Fletcher in Edinburgh North in 1970 he had narrowly won the then very marginal Edinburgh Central in February 1974.

It would be fair to say that he had a reputation as a radical left winger. He had come into politics through unilateralism. But he was never an identikit left wing figure. He had been against entry into the EEC in 1966. So were many left wingers, but then so was I.

Robin Cook's opposition to the Labour Party's plans for Scottish Devolution in the late 1970s marks him out as his own man on the left. Generally the left of the Labour Party in Scotland believed devolution could be a key step towards a Socialist Scottish state (it still could).

But there was another strand of opinion which saw Labour's plans as divisive, in the sense they could split the unity of the

British and International Socialist movement. In so far as he belonged to any particular group, that seemed to be an important part of Robin Cook's thinking. Yet Robin Cook has moved from being a somewhat marginal left wing figure to centre stage in Tony Blair's party, which is by any standard the most right wing Labour Party in history.

How has this happened? It can be summarised extremely simply and in two ways.

First, the turning point was his position in masterminding Neil Kinnock's campaign for the Labour Party Leadership. He was reputedly extremely good at it. And the campaign was successful.

In politics success breeds success and that success put Robin Cook into a different league. He was then a figure with whom everyone had to reckon.

Second is the simple word ability. Much press comment on Robin Cook has concentrated on his alleged aloofness. *Crossbencher's* famous description that he "looks like a garden gnome" has stuck. The idea that such a description would undermine his standing among the electorate has always seemed to me absurd. People like garden gnomes.

But if he is aloof, or whatever, why has he done so outstandingly well, year after year, in the Shadow Cabinet elections? After all, the Shadow Cabinet elections are a notorious opportunity for Labour MPs to get their own back for personal slights. Part of the explanation may lie in the fact that while Robin Cook may or may not have any personal political friends, he does not have any personal enemies.

But the key is the word ability.

He is also a consummate parliamentarian. Robin Cook's dispatch box performances have been well recorded. The best description comes from Edward Pearce in the *Sunday Times*, hardly a supporter of the left wing flame – "a talent for controlled contempt and a grasp of the details." A grasp of the details is what effective politics is all about.

My first parliamentary experience of Robin Cook was in the first Finance Bill Committee of the 1979–83 Parliament. The issue was a complex one about the taxation of Scotch whisky which is about much more than simply the level of duty. I had read all the briefs and was called to speak first from the backbenches. There was nothing at all wrong with the well informed competent speech I made – especially for a backbencher.

But Robin Cook's speech next, quietly delivered without histrionics, was in a different class. To be fair, he had been familiar with the issue for some time. But he went incisively to the heart of the issue, and wasted no words, an attribute of few parliamentary speeches.

When I was the Scottish New Towns Minister I had meetings with the five New Towns MPs, especially after the wind-up programme had been announced. All five Scottish Labour MPs attended and they were all very well informed and had always done their homework.

But one had onerous front bench duties – Robin Cook. Yet he tended to be the one who would say something like, "Minister, I am a little unclear as to how Paragraph 21(b) of the circular your department issued two weeks ago on this subject relates to the circular of eighteen months ago."

There are a number of rooms in the House Of Commons Library where Members work. In the innermost one, the rule is absolute silence. It is therefore occupied by only two categories of MPs. There are those who are working extremely hard and want above all no interruptions of any sort. And there are those who want a quiet doze. I have seen Robin Cook there many times. He was never having a quiet doze. That is the secret of his success.

## Norman Hogg

My predecessor, the late Betty Harvie Anderson gave me a great deal of advice. Most of it, to my benefit, I accepted. Some, to my regret, I did not follow. In every case, her advice has subsequently been proved extremely sound.

I shall always remember Betty telling me over a cup of tea one afternoon, "Allan, I expect you will win. Above all things you must get a pair. Leave the thank you letters for a day or two – the priority is a pair".

"What, Betty," I asked in my innocence, "is a pair?"

She explained – at length. A pair means that two MPs, one in Government and one in Opposition can agree not to vote on less high profile occasions (two line whips).

Essentially, we usually both go home thankfully to our respective beds or constituencies and the Government's majority does not change. Since the recent reforms following Michael Jopling's report, the position on late nights in the House of Commons has improved. Having a pair is particularly important for Scottish Members of Parliament, since we have Monday, Thursday and Friday commitments in our constituencies.

Forewarned by Betty Harvie Anderson, I met Norman Hogg in an STV studio around lunch time the day after the 1979 General Election. We were there with John Maxton, who had gained Cathcart from Teddy Taylor, for a programme about the new Scottish MPs.

In the event, the Cathcart result dominated the programme so that Norman and I were left to deal with each other and I raised the question of pairing. Norman was as vague about the concept as I had been when Betty Harvie Anderson raised it with me , but agreed to give it a try. A week later he congratulated me on my initiative – he had received some twenty-three letters from newly elected Tory MPs asking him to pair.

The relationship between pairs is purely personal – the political views of the two people involved are irrelevant. Very occasionally the pairing relationship comes into the public eye – usually when it has broken down.

One occasion illustrates it well. When the question of Ron Brown's suspension after an incident with the mace was being discussed in a full and fraught House of Commons, there arose from the Government benches that splendid Conservative figure Sir Nicholas Bonsor.

Ron Brown, he told the the House, was a man of extremely poor judgement. "After all," he added, "the Hon Member pairs with me." All sides of the House roared with laughter.

The atmosphere changed. From then on there was no question of any excessive penalty being imposed on Ron Brown.

The key to the relationship is complete trust. If you agree not to vote, you must not under any circumstances break the agreement. Of course misunderstanding can occur, but I am happy to say that since 1979 Norman and I have never let each other or the whips down.

Once we knowingly both voted the wrong way. It was on the Third Reading of a bill on embryo research. The Government were on a three line whip, although it was not fundamentally a partisan issue.

I asked Norman how he was going to vote. "You will be delighted to know Allan, that I intend to vote with the Government".

"That will do very nicely Norman", I replied, "because I intend to vote against the Government," and we did.

Norman is steeped in his Labour traditions – Christian Socialism and trade unionism. His late father was a trade union official and Lord Provost of Aberdeen. Norman is a devout Christian and an active elder in the Church of Scotland.

Christian socialism and being a church elder of the Kirk might suggest a dour personality. Nothing could be further from the truth. Norman has a dry, Aberdonian sense of humour, including about religion.

He kindly agreed in 1992 to accompany me to the Europartenariat in Thessaloniki. A Europartenariat is a very worthwhile European Union initiative at which, in a very organised way, small firms from the regions of Europe (and beyond) have excellent opportunities to establish trading links. We were lobbying for a Europartenariat in Glasgow (eventually successfully).

On the first evening we were being well entertained by our Greek hosts. Somewhat late on one of them, in expansive frame of mind, announced to the gathering, "This Europartenariat is the best thing that ever happened to the people of Thessaloniki."

"Well, " said Norman "They did once receive a letter from St Paul."

Long pause.

"To which I understand they have not yet replied!"

Norman Hogg's negotiating background suited him admirably for the Whip's office when he rose to Deputy Chief Whip 1985-1987 (an elected position).

He lost by one vote to Derek Foster in a contest for the position of Chief Whip (to considerable surprise) and resigned over lack of consultation. There followed a short period on the Scottish Opposition front bench where Norman fell foul of certain educational interests and their press contacts (I know the feeling well).

Then he took up what many feel to be his natural role in the House of Commons – as a member of the Chairman's Panel since 1988. As a Chairman of the Committees, including the whole House of Commons, his sense of fairness and humour stand him in good stead. He has an excellent knack of defusing situations. Members feel that it is bad form to create unnecessary trouble when Norman is in the Chair.

In politics, the wheel turns but often in unexpected ways. On the face of it however, Norman Hogg could be an outstanding candidate for a Deputy Speakership should there be vacancies in a future Parliament. That of course would make life suddenly difficult for me.

You can't pair with a Deputy Speaker!

**Margaret Ewing**

British Politics is supposed, by some, to be run by an unfairly dominant male elite. Strange then that two political parties should have had at the same time women parliamentary leaders of the same name – Margaret.

Margaret Thatcher's and Margaret Ewing's political beliefs are fundamentally opposed. But as politicians, and at the risk of offending both of them, they have certain characteristics in common.

Some women in politics display a feminine abrasiveness in their relations with men. What *Private Eye* describes as the "wimmin's lobby" often appear to regard men as the main enemy in political life. The 'woman's right to choose' movement which now so sadly dominates the Labour Party is their key triumph. The woman has the right to choose but the baby has the right only to die, is their cry. It is not an attractive phenomenon.

Margaret Ewing, like Margaret Thatcher, is quite different. Both are determined women, both are attractive and both will readily bestow winning feminine smiles on men in order to help win a point of argument. They are also both meticulous about their dress – and use it to make a political point. Margaret Ewing naturally favours the SNP's yellow and black. Having an excellent figure (and the famous legs) does help.

Politically her position appears to have shifted to some extent, reflecting her own constituency. Margaret Ewing represented East Dumbartonshire from 1974–79.

One of the most controversial things she did was to persuade the SNP MPs to abstain rather than vote against the Labour Government's Bill to nationalise the shipbuilding and aviation industries. That may have represented the views of many workers in East Dumbartonshire. It is very hard to see the MP for Moray taking similar action.

The attitude of SNP MPs towards Westminster varies. On the one hand their political lives are dedicated to the demise of the United Kingdom Parliament. They do not want to be there at all; they want to be members of a separate institution in an independent Scotland. On the other hand the House of Commons and its Scottish Committees are important platforms. The substantial Scottish press and broadcasting corps at Westminster must produce stories and comment for the folks back home – and the national media take an intermittent interest in Scottish Affairs. Scottish delegations lobby Scottish MPs; SNP MPs have constituents with their individual problems and concerns.

Since 1979 there have always been only a small number of SNP Members of Parliament. Margaret Ewing, the SNP Parliamentary Leader (Alex Salmond being Party Leader) has not seemed to find the potential dilemmas a problem. There is no doubt she enjoys being in Parliament. This is in contrast to, for example, Jim Sillars. Jim Sillars on occasion was a highly effective master of parliamentary procedure. But he gave the very strong impression that he did not like Westminster. Membership was an undesirable necessity.

Margaret, outgoing and gregarious with a ready turn of wit, is a natural. Her political record points to her position as doubtful about extra-parliamentary activity. At the time of the rise of the SNP's '79 Group in 1982 she warned about the dangers of the SNP being like a rent-a-mob.

Parliamentary work at Westminster is not in practice mainly about questions and speeches on the floor of the House of Commons although that is where attention is usually focused. The real hours are spent in Committee. Margaret Ewing works hard at putting down practical amendents to Government Bills. She put down, for example, a large number to the Scottish School Boards Bill in 1988. Michael Forsyth, a Minister often more in charge of his brief than the brief itself, has always appeared to particularly respect her contributions and has often accepted practical amendments put forward by Margaret.

It is not always easy for a representative of a small party to make an impact on the House of Commons (although it could be argued that the Rev Ian Paisley does not appear to have a problem). The Commons above all appreciates wit, clarity and brevity. This is not surprising. Most speeches in the Commons are dull, obscure and far too long. Margaret Ewing is listened to. She seldom goes over the top in yah-boo politics. How would she fare in a devolutionary or independent Parliament? A hypothetical question impossible to answer. But she is certainly effective in the Parliament we have.

### Michael Heseltine

Michael Heseltine has been to an Eastwood Conservative Dinner – when he was on the backbenches. He made a typically splendid barnstorming speech, shook hands with everyone, then came home to stay with Susie and me afterwards. We sat chatting when he suddenly asked, "Why do you think people like us are in politics, Allan?" I gave some vague, half baked answer.

"No," he commented. "It is because we have twice as much energy as most people."

That is the real clue to Michael. It is hardly surprising his own book is entitled *Where there's a will*.

We first met in 1975 when Michael was leading the Tory assault against Tony Benn's interventionist industrial policy and I was working on the CBI's response. His energy and enthusiasm created a real belief in a somewhat shell-shocked business world that this particular battle could be won. It was, when Harold Wilson saw what was happening and acted to head off trouble, being the master tactician he always was.

Much of course has been written about Michael Heseltine's challenge against Margaret Thatcher in 1990. I was the 'candidate's friend' to the Conservative candidates in the Paisley byelections at the time – the admirable John Workman and Ewan Marwick, so tragically killed in Russia not long after.

Michael was due to speak in Paisley Town Hall two days after he announced his candidature. I spoke to Michael, to party bosses and to the candidates. Everyone was in something of a quandary.

Should Michael come, would he, what would he say about the Prime Minister? I told the candidates – it's your campaign and finally, your decision. My advice was unequivocal – confirm the invitation. Michael Heseltine will be brilliant, he won't rock the boat, and he will fill Paisley Town Hall. He was, he didn't and he did.

It was a great, old style political meeting. And the Tory vote held up in the byelections.

It is a great myth that Michael Heseltine is disliked or distrusted by the Tory right. The market men voted for Margaret Thatcher on the first ballot in the leadership contest in 1990. But on the second, some voted unequivocally for Michael. Many others hesitated. They took the view that Michael had been absolutely honest. He had exercised his right to put his name forward.

Michael Heseltine resigned from Margaret Thatcher's Cabinet over Westland helicopters. Most people, including me, found the issues a bit puzzling. Now he is Deputy Prime Minister. The future? Who knows? But he is the greatest Tory campaigner of them all.

### A Knight of the Scottish Shires

The Tories have never been the London party. In the eighteenth century, Tories were rightly described as 'The Country Party'. In Margaret Thatcher's years, the symbol was Essex Man. The most significant result early on the night of the 1992 General Election was Basildon – a Conservative hold. There is a strong link between the Country Party of the eighteenth century and Essex Man – a suspicion of the pretensions of the metropolitan elite.

When I was elected in 1979 I was in a sense returning to London, where I had happily worked for many years. I was invited to many parties by courteous and pleasant people. They, naturally enough, asked me what I thought of Margaret Thatcher. After a pause I would reply, "Margaret Thatcher is a dangerous figure!" Nods of approval! "Far too left wing, far too left wing," I would add sadly. Appalled silence. In the West of Scotland everyone would have laughed – the London elite takes itself much too seriously.

The long held Conservative scepticism about the metropolitan elite is best expressed in that most traditional of terms, 'The Knights of The Shires'. In practice the term is less important because the shires are less important electorally. Modern Conservatism is predominately suburban. Nevertheless the concept of 'The Knights of The Shires' goes to the heart of the Tory party. It means tradition, commitment, loyalty and independence of thought. Strange though it may seem, the St Andrews free marketeers – radical and new – have seldom had problems with 'The Knights of The Shires' tradition, except over agricultural policy perhaps. Douglas Mason's campaigns in Glenrothes Rimbleton, for example, described in an earlier chapter, were mainly financed by the independents – not on the whole 'Knights' but certainly the 'Shires'.

The modern Conservative party ignores the values embodied by the phrase 'The Knights of The Shires' at its peril. There is only one Scottish MP at present who really embodies that tradition – Sir Hector Monro. That is not to decry the value and commitment of the others. One swithers on Lord James Douglas-Hamilton. He represents all the traditions and values of 'The Knights of The Shires'. Stories of his personal courtesy to people in all walks of life are legion. They are also true. As a politician, Lord James is much under-estimated. His pleasant demeanour masks an iron will. His public commitment was demonstrated when he gave up his personal right to be Earl of Selkirk. On the day in question, James was due to answer an adjournment debate. He could not do so because he was arguably a member of the House of Lords. I did it – no problem, but James in the midst of this complex family situation took the trouble to explain to me fully the background to the debate. In terms of background, values and commitment, Lord James qualifies as a 'Knight of The Shires'. But Edinburgh West, which he so assiduously and meticulously represents, is patently not a shire seat.

The concept of a 'Knight of The Shires' is essentially one about backbenchers. So the two Scottish Office Junior Ministers, George Kynoch and Raymond Robertson do not in any event qualify. That is not in any way to under-estimate their place in political history. My own view is that they have excellent futures ahead. George and Raymond are both able Ministers. They and Phil Gallie had arguably the best Conservative results in the 1992 General Election (apart from Eastwood!). Without question, they changed the face of British politics. The Union might have been dead until Kincardine and Deeside and Aberdeen South came in for the Unionists.

Phil Gallie has been described by *The Guardian* as "the thinking man's Rab C. Nesbitt" and since it was *The Guardian* Phil is rather proud of the fact. His victory in Ayr in 1992 stunned commentators and opponents alike. He was certainly aided by one indomitable Scottish Tory knight, Sir Albert McQuarrie. In the middle of the election campaign Sir Albert laid a bet, "a substantial sum to show my faith in the Party", with an Ayr bookie that the Scots Tories would end up with more MPs after the election than before. He received odds of 100-1.

But Phil is much more in the tradition of Teddy Taylor than 'The Knights of The Shires'. He has particularly strong views on law and order. Although heavily involved in fisheries policies, his constituency and background are more urban than rural. Phil Gallie is currently Vice Chairman of the Scottish Conservative Party and shares with 'The Knights of The Shires' a high degree of Party loyalty. Since I share an office with Phil, I can attest to his formidable and proactive work rate. Whatever Phil Gallie works on it is with dedication, commitment and enthusiasm. A tremendous asset to the Party, especially in the West of Scotland, but not a 'Knight of The Shires'.

That beautiful county, Perthshire has produced two Conservative MPs since 1979. Sir Nicholas Fairbairn and Bill Walker. Of Nicky everyone who knew him has memories and stories. The title of his autobiography, sadly incomplete on his death, *A Life Is Too Short* really summed Nicky up. Tributes to Nicky Fairbairn have been paid by all. The attendance at his Memorial Service was itself perhaps the best tribute to a remarkable and remarkably talented man. His resignation as Solicitor General for Scotland was entirely due to his having unwisely answered the telephone to a journalist he did not know early in the morning. I always thought Nicky should subsequently have been reinstated to the Government, although not as a law officer. Nicky at his best had a mastery of the English language without peer in recent Parliaments except perhaps, in a rather different way, Enoch Powell.

Nicky was always his own man, as is the other Perthshire Tory, Bill Walker. North Tayside is very much a 'Shire Seat' but no one, least of all Bill would describe him as a potential 'Knight of The Shires'. Indeed he was once famously described by *The Scotsman* as having "probably caused the Scottish Office more aggro than any member of the opposition parties". Bill has been uncompromising in his views, especially on the Union and on Europe and is an astute user of Parliamentary procedure on behalf of his constituents interests – whether Scotch Whisky, raspberries, reed cultivation or the rating of caravans.

But there is only one Scottish Tory MP who represents everything that is meant by the concept of 'The Knights of The Shires', and a great deal more. Sir Hector Monro is now well into his fourth decade as the Member of Parliament for Dumfries, formerly Dumfriesshire. He joined the then Dumfriesshire Unionist Association fifty years ago and served as a Dumfriesshire County Councillor for fifteen years. His roots are deep in the community he represents.

The greatest tragedy to hit that community was of course the Lockerbie Air Disaster. The world saw and heard Hector's words of simple dignity at the American Memorial Service when he stood side by side with President Clinton. In the House, on the night of the Lockerbie Disaster, Brian Wilson, not one readily given to handing out plaudits to Tories, described Hector's obvious anguish as "the mark of a man who is truly part of the community he represents."

The modern intake of Members of Parliament on both sides of the House is often criticised not for its expertise or hard work, but for the excessive number of professional politicians. Many feel that our democratic representatives should have a broader background than those who have gone the route of University–Researcher–Parliament with little or no experience of what some describe as the 'real world', however imprecise that term might be. Nothing could be more real than flying with the RAF in World War II. Hector, then a student, volunteered at the age of 18. As a former Spitfire Pilot (with 603 Squadron) he is held in enormous respect by the RAF who have made him an Air Commodore and Inspector General of the Royal Auxiliary Air Force.

Most MPs have a personal sporting interest. Few if any have the range of Hector's. In the world of sport he is best known as a former President of the Scottish Rugby Union and for his interests in the country sports and motoring. It was strongly rumoured in the Scottish Office that on occasion he took over the driving of the official car, covering the miles between Edinburgh and Kirtle-bridge in a rather shorter time than was customary. Sir Hector's front bench experience goes back almost thirty years – he was appointed Scottish Whip in 1967.

Most believed he had settled for the role of senior and respected backbencher after he left Margaret Thatcher's Government in 1981. When he returned to the Scottish Office in 1992 it was widely felt that he was doing John Major and Ian Lang a considerable favour. There were raised eyebrows that he was not made a Minister of State. This was no disrespect to the admirable and amiable Peter Fraser (Lord Fraser of Carmyllie). But there was precedent for two Ministers of State at the Scottish Office. In practice it proved an inspired move. In charge of Agriculture, Fisheries and the Environment, Sir Hector had the great advantage of the respect and knowledge of the communities he had to deal with. He set himself a schedule which would have been punishing for a man half his age. Presumably because of his farming background, he arrived at the office early. He often muttered darkly about the lifestyle of Ministers who did not turn up until the advanced hour of 8.45am (me!).

Despite his own workload he took a lively interest across a broad range of subjects where his shrewdness and common sense were of great help. He often took an independent but successful line – on water disconnections and sleeper services for example.

Civil servants often try to persuade doubtful or recalcitrant

Ministers by quoting precedent. It was a tactic to be tried at their peril with Sir Hector Monro. He could quote from personal experience going back to when they were babes in arms. Sir Hector Monro is retiring at the next General Election. No doubt he will wish to relax a bit. But it is impossible to believe that this particular 'Knight of The Shires' will be wholly lost to Scottish public life. I am sure there will be further chapters in a most distinguished and selfless career of public service.

## Teddy Taylor

Teddy Taylor is a Glaswegian, born and bred, with politics in his soul. By the age of 23 he was already a member of Glasgow City Council. Five years later he was Member of Parliament for Cathcart, a difficult seat with a small majority. He was able to hang on to the seat against the odds longer than anyone would have thought possible through his very personal populist approach. He was also helped, it should be said, by a superlative constituency organisation with people like John Young and Derek and Jeanette Mason. His unashamedly right-wing views, particularly on crime and vandalism, undoubtedly struck a chord with the ordinary grass roots Glasgow voter.

When the Conservatives returned to power in 1970, he was appointed one of the Junior Ministers in the Scottish Office. But Teddy was soon to show that he did not back populist causes for the sake of his own personal popularity. His views reflected his own deeply held political beliefs. Who else within a year of achieving his first Government Office would risk ruining his future career by resigning in principle over Britain's application to join the Common Market – and do so from a Government led by that arch-European, Ted Heath? Surprisingly perhaps, the difference of opinion was patched up in time for Teddy to return briefly to the Scottish Office before the unwisely called February 1974 General Election brought the Heath Government to its premature end.

In Opposition after Margaret Thatcher came out firmly against a Scottish Assembly, Teddy became Shadow Secretary of

State for Scotland. I recall one meeting between CBI Scotland and the Scottish Opposition team. Teddy was extraordinarily impressive. Industrialists are not on the whole urban populists. What struck everyone was Teddy's grasp of detail on a whole range of issues of concern to Scottish business and industry. His role in the 1979 campaign against Labour's Scottish Assembly proposals was crucial. Many of the NO campaigners frankly did not believe we could win. Teddy, displaying his customary energy and enthusiasm never for one moment wavered in his belief that the YES campaign was on the run.

It was Teddy's misfortune that after the referendums in Scotland and Wales had brought down the Callaghan Government, Margaret Thatcher led the Conservatives back to power in 1979, Cathcart finally fell to Labour. A combination of population movements and a well-organised Labour campaign in its strong areas like Castlemilk overcame Teddy's outstanding reputation as a formidable constituency MP. He was not to be kept away from Westminster for long. Within a year he was back in the House representing Southend East. That English seaside resort is completely unlike urban Glasgow. But people are people and Teddy is Teddy. Having canvassed for him in the byelection and spoken in Southend East subsequently, I know how much he is respected there. His non-stop constituency role clearly came as something of a shock to the good folks of Southend, used to a rather quieter and laid back Conservative approach. But getting major improvements in the standard of the train carriages to London is hugely important to Southend commuters. Teddy achieved that single handed.

Iain Sproat tells the story of speaking in Southend when the announcement was made. Teddy received a standing ovation. Iain told me, "In Scotland all that would have happened was people saying, 'Aye, not before time.'"

Politics is ultimately about power in its various manifestations. Many MPs do not particularly wish to be Ministers for long periods. But there are few who could reasonably aspire to Cabinet level and who consistently deny themselves that power because of a principle. Teddy is one of those few. His position on Europe, even before he resigned from office in 1991 and ever since has been clear, consistent and unequivocal. It seemed to me at the time, and I said so to everyone who would listen, that it was absurd to deprive Teddy of the party whip on a vote on Europe. How else would he ever have voted?

Further, while electors do not always know the views of their MPs (or often care very much), everyone who voted for Teddy in Southend East could hardly have avoided knowing where he stood on the European issue.

When the whip was withdrawn, I saw Teddy and gave him a note. It said simply how sorry I was and any time his constituency wanted a Government Minister to speak I would be delighted to oblige. Happily that particular problem was resolved when the Whip was restored.

Teddy is a natural political campaigner. In June 1989 he barnstormed around that part of Glasgow Central he had previously represented during the byelection campaign. People were stopping him in the streets to shake him warmly by the hand – not in my experience a common phenomenon for Tories in Glasgow. He will doubtless continue to be a thorn in the flesh of the Euro-fanatics. He has been effective in that capacity – for example, when in 1990 he pointed out that the EC was then spending some £600million to subsidise the growth of poor quality, high tar tobacco, then dumping the resultant product on Africa.

One never knows in politics but Sir Teddy Taylor seems happy with the freedom of speech the backbenches gives him. Brussels must hope he quietly fades away, but I believe his unique, urgent, Glaswegian eloquence will be heard a long time yet on behalf of his constituents and the interests of the people of the United Kingdom.

## CHAPTER 15

# LOCKERBIE

In common with everyone else I could not fail to be touched by the horrendous human carnage of the Lockerbie bombing but my Ministerial responsibilities at the Scottish Office did not involve me directly in the outrage.

However as time passed and the stalemate continued between our own Crown Office, US State Department and Libya I became concerned as Minister with responsibility for Industry about the effects our sanctions policy was having on businesses in this country.

It was clear that we were playing by the rules but other countries were not. Italy, I believe, is clearly breaking the sanctions, and worse still, American companies are avoiding the impact of sanctions by using South Korean companies.

Within Government circles these arguments did not cut much ice. The Crown Office argued very strongly that the evidence pointed strongly to the two Libyan suspects and that the only way out of sanctions was for the Libyan Government to deliver the two suspects for trial in Scotland or the USA.

Following my return to the backbenches in February 1995 I was invited by the Islamic Council of Scotland to visit Libya. During my time as Industry Minister at the Scottish Office I had been approached on a number of occasions by Asian and Pakistani business people in the West of Scotland saying that they could see no resolution to the affair. The Islamic Council had the same fears, and I agreed to go to Libya in April of that year.

It was not arranged in advance that I would see Col Gadaffi, but meetings were arranged with a number of high ranking Government officials. After I had several meetings with officials I was informed that Col Gadaffi would see me.

We drove for an hour into the desert from Tripoli, and to be honest I have really no idea of the location of the Libyan Head of State. The hour long meeting took place in a tent, a rather luxurious tent I have to admit. We spoke through his interpreter who was a Professor who had taught at an American university.

There was only a small group present during the meeting. A few Libyan officials and Mr Tufail Mohammed Shaheen MBE, President of the Glasgow Mosque were present.

Col Gadaffi put forward very sophisticated arguments as to why he could not agree to the Scottish Crown Office demands or those of the United States State Department. I gained the impression that he would have liked to have found a solution to the problem and establish normal relations with the United Kingdom and the United States.

The Libyans did not use my meeting with Col Gadaffi for propaganda purposes. It was reported in their press and on television that a meeting had taken place between Col Gadaffi and a visiting British MP.

Col Gadaffi has since said that he is willing to allow the two suspects to be tried by a Scottish court in another country. I personally support this idea which was first mooted I believe by Professor Robert Black.

Following my meeting with him Col Gadaffi made this offer through adverts in the American press. Unfortunately the idea of a Scottish trial being held outside the country in perhaps say, The Hague was rejected by the Government, and totally ruled out by the Labour Party. I believe we have to try and put ourselves in the position of the Libyans. Would we force two of our citizens to stand trial in a foreign country which had enabled a foreign power to bomb us, and with which we not only had no extradition treaty and also no diplomatic relations?

The Libyans are worried that their citizens would not receive a fair trial in the atmosphere which would surround the occasion and although I believe that this concern is not fully justified, we have to understand their fears that if their citizens were found not guilty in a Scottish court that they could find themselves being picked up outside the High Court in Edinburgh by the CIA and taken for another trial in America.

I believe that this would not necessarily happen.

The Scottish Crown Office and the American State Department are supposed to be two separate organisations but it seems odd that when both issued statements about my suggestion regarding a trial in front of a Scottish court in another country, the statement issued by both was identical.

This among other things leads me to believe that there is collusion between the Crown Office and the CIA. It has to be suspicious that we are in this stand-off position and that the British Government appear to be doing nothing about the problem.

This is not the place to go into all the arguments but it is strange that on the day of the tragedy, so many Americans arrived so quickly on the scene. Nor have Tam Dalyell's insistent questions about the warnings that were given ever been satisfactorily answered.

I was concerned by the reaction to my visit and my support for the proposal that a Scottish court should sit outside Scotland.

A number of suggestions appeared in the media that somehow I had a financial interest in putting forward such proposals. I have friends in the Asian and Pakistini communities, most of whom are in my constituency but I have no financial interests at all.

According to the media the Crown Office were concerned by my involvement and it is a fact that I was charged with my breach of the peace offence over the M77 protest on the eve of travelling to Libya. The timing of my being charged was strange. Nothing had happened for some considerable time despite my solicitor's enquiries. Other people have suggested that the two are connected but there is nothing to prove this.

The idea of a Scottish trial abroad is still being pursued and Tam Dalyell, who has a thorough knowledge of this issue, has continued to pursue the matter through Parliament.

With Tam's permission, I intervened in an adjournment debate he had managed to achieve and asked what are sanctions supposed to be achieving? The issue is not going to go away. There are too many questions unanswered.

I have no regrets about visiting Libya. Something has to be done to try and bring this episode to an end for the sake of the relatives of those who died. During my week-long visit to Libya I met many senior officials. They are a very sophisticated and intelligent people. The country has a long history and at one time was the granary of the Roman Empire. There are remains of Roman sites throughout the land.

In addition to the suffering of the relatives of those who perished the present stalemate is helping no one. Our firms are losing out and meanwhile no moves appear to be being made to resolve the situation. But there are a lot of people still endeavouring to find the answers.

Since returning from Libya I have kept my contacts with business interests in the country so that I may be in a position to assist our country to establish proper trading links when normal relationships are re-established.

CHAPTER 16
# THE MARKET MEN MARCH ON

The 1960s and 70s at St Andrews marked a watershed in the University's involvement in national politics. Before then there had been one St Andrews graduate in Beresford Craddock, a little known Tory MP in the Lloyd George era. Afterwards there were several, some to become important national figures. Not all of them were Conservatives, of course, since the intellectual atmosphere created by the St Andrews University Conservative Association had its impact on the other parties. But the majority were Conservatives. At present there are St Andrews graduates in all four major Scottish political parties.

John MacGregor, MP for South Norfolk and former Minister of Agriculture, Secretary of State for Education and Science and

Leader of the House of Commons, had graduated the year before I went up but he had had the same tuition in political economy and modern history. Although not perhaps as rigorous a supporter of the free market as his later St Andrean colleagues his sympathies were certainly in the right place. Before even entering Parliament he identified Edward Heath's February 1972 contribution to the miners as the first of his 'U-turns' and the beginning of the end of his government. Early in his ministerial career, as 'Minister for Small Businesses' he was responsible for abolishing thirty powers of entry into and inspection of small businesses. Later, as Minister of Agriculture, he tried to cut farm subsidies, achieve tighter controls over farming expenditure and bring about major reforms in the Common Agricultural Policy. As Education Secretary he successfully introduced student loans.

John Marshall, MP for Hendon South and former MEP for North London was a contemporary, also studying under Professors Nisbet and Gash. It was from him that I picked up the baton in Dundee East where he had fought the seat in 1964 and 1966. Two years later he was a member of Aberdeen City Council where he served a spell as chairman of the Transport Committee, an experience which made him a convinced supporter of bus privatisation. After a move to London he promptly gained a seat on Ealing Borough Council, serving a term as chairman of its Local Services Committee. He describes himself as a passionate believer in the Social Market economy and, though a supporter of the European Commission, warned against joining the Exchange Rate Mechanism, a warning that in due course was to prove more than amply justified. He is a member of the 'No Turning Back Group'.

Robert Jones, MP for West Herefordshire and Minister of State for the Environment was among my students in the last period before I left St Andrews to move to London. I doubt if I can therefore claim much credit for his development into a classical product of the St Andrews University Conservative Association, anti-nationalisation, pro-privatisation and in favour of letting the market sort out problems like pollution.

His own studies, ambition and the influence of others have

combined to do that. A town councillor while still a student, he fought his first parliamentary election immediately upon graduating. A dedicated canvasser and student of local election results, he is also a member of the No Turning Back Group.

Michael Fallon, MP for Darlington from 1983 to the last General Election belonged to a later generation still of St Andrews students but his commitment to free market thought was no less fervent. Despite representing a seat in the North of England he made no attempt to hide his hostility to regional aid and was noted for his views that what is needed in depressed areas like the North was more private and less public investment. A member of the No Turning Back Group.

Chris Chope, MP for Southampton from 1983 to the last General Election was actually a student at Dundee in the days when it was part of St Andrews University. I first met him when he gave valuable help in the Hilltown local election and in my own campaign in Dundee East. He went on to lead the radical Conservative group in the London Borough of Wandsworth before bringing a typical St Andrews-style ideological zeal to the House of Commons. Member of the No Turning Back Group.

Michael Forsyth, MP for Stirling since 1983, entered the House of Commons at the same time as Michael Fallon but belongs to an even younger generation of St Andrews' graduates. Entering St Andrews as a socialist he became a convinced believer in the merits of private enterprise and individual freedom of choice. Before entering Parliament he had set out the ways this philosophy could be applied in practice both through his membership of Westminster City Council and in a series of pamphlets. In Parliament he used his early years on the back benches to argue for the practical application of what by then had become known as Thatcherite views over a wide range of political problems. He has a capacity that is commented on elsewhere.

John Ward, MP for Poole is a St Andrews graduate of an earlier generation, before the Conservative Association achieved its radical reputation. He entered the House at the same time as I did and certainly holds views that would not be out of place among his younger ex-St Andrews colleagues. In an early rebellion he demanded tougher action against 'closed shops'. He attacked direct-labour organisations, supported early privatisation and backed calls for abolition of the rent acts. He is currently Parliamentary Private Secretary to the Prime Minister – John Major's eyes and ears in the House of Commons.

It would be misleading to imply that St Andrews graduates are entirely confined to the Conservative benches of the House of Commons. Each of the opposition parties contains a former student or two. Labour's Lewis Moonie, who represents Adam Smith's birthplace of Kirkcaldy, can often be seen wearing his graduate tie, as can SNP leader, Alex Salmond and the Liberal Democrats' former Scottish Leader, Malcolm Bruce. Indeed, had Malcolm Bruce remained leader of the Scottish Liberal Democrats then all political parties in Scotland would currently be led by former St Andrews University students. For George Robertson, the Shadow Secretary of State, was at Queen's College, Dundee before it parted company with St Andrews to become Dundee University.

Since politics, like nature, abhors a vacuum, it is not surprising that a high degree of political activity by one party in an institution stimulates activity by others. But the emergence of St Andrews graduates in the other political parties represents more individual enterprise than a continuing phenomenon.

Leaving aside John Ward and John McGregor of a slightly more senior generation, every other St Andrean who became a Conservative MP also was invited to join the No Turning Back Group. Those of us who ended up as Members of Parliament were a minority. Most of the student activists of my generation put politics aside when they graduated and settled down to pursue careers in more traditional occupations.

There was however another group who continued to pursue the ideas developed at St Andrews more through influencing the political process than through directly participating in it. Foremost among them was Dr Madsen Pirie. After a spell in the USA working for the Republican Study Committee and teaching at Hillsdale College, he returned to Britain to found the Adam Smith

Institute, over the past twenty years undoubtedly the most influential and stimulating of Britain's think tanks. His principal assistants in this project were the Butler brothers, Stuart and Eamonn. After graduating Stuart had worked for a year at Swinton Conservative College before joining Madsen Pirie at Hillsdale where they planned the new institute. Eamonn meanwhile, had taken Madsen Pirie's old job with the Republican Study Committee. Once Madsen and Stuart had got this institute up and running, Eamonn Butler returned from the USA to help build it to its present position of influence while Stuart Butler returned to Washington to work for the Heritage Foundation, a larger and longer established American equivalent of the Adam Smith Institute. He is now its Deputy Director.

Another character was Stephen Eyres. Like Stuart Butler he spent some time as a tutor at Swinton Conservative College. He will be best remembered however, for his time with the Freedom Association editing its newspapers, including a special strike-breaking edition that sold a quarter of a million copies during the 1980 'day of action'.

Electioneering activity by the St Andrews Group – real politics – had started with Douglas Mason, he of Glenrothes Rimbleton fame. Douglas still lives in Glenrothes where he has been a meticulously hard working member of the New Town Development Corporation. He is now Domestic Policy Adviser to the Adam Smith Institute and has assisted with research for among others, Michael Forsyth and myself. He is seldom seen without his graduate tie. Unusually for the group, he studied science at St Andrews not arts. One of his many publications has ensured its honoured place in the mythology of the left. *Revising the Rating System* (published by the Adam Smith Institute) argued for a poll tax well before the idea became current. Others were putting forward similar views but it is not for nothing that Douglas Mason has been described as the father of the poll tax. Whether he would have implemented it in the same way as it was done is another matter.

Some of Douglas Mason's other publications have also been

obviously influential. I relied heavily on his *Time to Call Time* when proposing my 1986 Private Member's Bill to reform the licensing laws in England and Wales on Scottish lines. That campaign was eventually successful. Partly successful was his *Shedding A Tier* – on local government. Not very successful was *The Quango Complex* on local government quango-type institutions. They seem to march on forever. Among others have been *Licensed To Live,* on restrictive controls and a precursor of Michael Heseltine's *Deregulation Initiative.*

Douglas Mason was also a major contributor to the 'Omega Project' which operated between 1981 and 1983. It consisted of a series of study groups to examine the activities of every government department and made recommendations on policy. These recommendations went to Ministers and the final report ran to over half a million words.

One suspects most recommendations were examined then quietly buried but that does not mean the exercise was futile. Those who want more of the taxpayer's money for this, that and the other are too often successful in their importuning. The political system responds to pressure. Those who argue for a limited although positive role for the state must constantly press counter arguments. Many think tanks, institutes, study groups and individuals constantly put policy suggestions before politicians and the public. Douglas Mason, Madsen Pirie and Eamonn Butler are not content merely to be the writers of booklets and the organisers of seminars. They are advocates, fully prepared to argue their case on radio and television. Public opinion is influenced by many things and since its foundation the Adam Smith Institute has undoubtedly had a continuing and influential role.

It is obvious from these short sketches that there has been a continuing link between St Andrews and the No Turning Back Group. In one respect the No Turning Back Group incorporates the key traditions established at St Andrews – the combination of intellectual free market ideas and hard nosed political action.

The Parliamentary Conservative Party abounds in groups which meet for political dinners. Some are eminently respectable such as the Unionist Club, which all former Conservative Ministers are entitled to join. Some are more formal than others, some more political than others. Membership of all is by invitation only. The best is perhaps the '92 Group', a large, fairly loose Centre-Right group formidably organised by the redoubtable Sir George Gardiner. Margaret Thatcher as Prime Minister attended a '92 Group' dinner and it is not for nothing that George Told her, "Prime Minister, we are your Praetorian guard."

The No Turning Back Group has never aspired to mass membership among the Parliamentary Party nor to organise the elections for back bench committees. Loyal supporters of Margaret Thatcher's, it is a matter of (more or less) public record that members of the NTB voted for all three candidates who stood for the succession. The NTB is about ideas. The NTB met initially under the Chairmanship of (who else?) Ralph, Lord Harris of High Cross. Originally in 1985 NTB was a wholly back bench group. I was invited to join on my resignation from Government in 1986. As events developed NTB members joined the Government and rose through the ranks. Three Secretaries of State in the present Cabinet are NTB members. The NTB joined the political and intellectual debate with the November 1985 publication *No Turning Back: a new agenda from a group of Conservative MPs*. Four were St Andreans and the theme was unequivocal – the only way for the Conservative Party was to go forward with our ideas, not to relapse and let Socialism dominate the agenda.

That view was published by the Conservative Political Centre, as have been the subsequent essays, with one exception. *Save Our Schools* with which Michael Forsyth was particularly associated, argued the case for extending parental choice and improving educational standards through what has become known as opting out (July 1986). In 1988 the NTB produced *The NHS: A Suitable Case For Treatment*, which examined the fundamental issues of how to finance the NHS and the relationship between the NHS and private practice.

In 1989 came *Europe: Onwards From Bruges* which examined European Community economic, competion trade and regional policies. Needless to say we (I was co-author) also examined the biggest racket the European Continent has ever seen – the Common Agricultural Policy. 1990 saw *Choice and Responsibility: the Welfare State*. As its title suggests this set out an agenda across a whole range of areas – social policy, health, education, law and order.

More recently, the challenge of Social Security has predominated the political agenda, across the political spectrum. Who can deny the immense contribution made by that impeccably, intellectually honest Labour figure Frank Field? The No Turning Back Group addressed the issues in *Who benefits? Reinventing Social Security*. Peter Lilley was not of course an author of that, but his approach to a vital area of reform reflects to some extent the *Who benefits?* approach.

The most recent NTB publication was not published by the CPC, nor co-authored by all back bench members. *A Conservative Europe 1994 and Beyond* was published by the European Foundation. It is a comprehensive and completely consistent account of how the European Union should develop from a free market viewpoint. Since on this occasion I was not a co-author it is not inappropriate to suggest that it should be required reading for every candidate standing in the Conservative cause at the next General Election.

In conclusion the St Andrews group has never been as close knit as the above analysis might at first glance suggest. Not all know each other personally particularly well, although all are acquainted. Every Member of Parliament operates in a much broader context than students of his or her university days.

Nor were free market ideas ever the sole preserve of our university. At the time St Andrews students were publishing their ideas in *Progressus*, the market economy, libertarian tradition was alive and well in universities up and down the land – notably for example in York.

At political level, it could be argued that the St Andrews contribution was merely one of among many, that what happened in that tiny university town and to its Conservative graduates was and is not a decisive factor in the political landscape now fashioned by what we know as Thatcherism.

In one sense that has to be correct. The massive intellectual and political contribution of Sir Keith Joseph was central to the climate and organisation in which Thatcherism thrived. St Andrews was always perhaps an irritant. But irritants have their uses. Irritants create pearls.

The tradition and principles of market forces have always been a force in Conservative thought. It unites with the 'Country Party' tradition in its scepticism about, and distrust of, the merits of centralising power in the state.

What makes the ex St Andrean MPs and the Adam Smith Institute so important is their continued and active presence. One can reasonably hope that those out of Parliament will soon return. The flow of practical ideas will continue from the Adam Smith Institute. It is all part of a wider and looser movement.

Few with sense confidently forecast the future of individual political careers. Chance plays too great a role. But it would be astonishing if at least some of the St Andreans mentioned did not have a major part to play in the future of the Conservative and Unionist Party and the country.

The future challenge for the market men is clear. In British politics, there must be both constant vigilance and constant inquiry into how market forces can be further effectively used to improve the standard of living and quality of our public services. The intellectual battle against state collectivism can never be finally won, but it is certainly going the way of the individualist. When did a member of the Shadow Cabinet praise socialism recently?

Yet the free marketeers, individually and together now face a darker, more subtle and more dangerous foe than British state collectivism – the centralising European state envisaged by so many in the European Union. The enemy of liberty is no longer London, the enemy is Brussels. The hardest part of the march is yet to come.

## CHAPTER 17

# PRIVATISATION

In my student days, Conservative governments paid lip service to rolling back the frontiers of the state; denationalisation as they called it then; privatisation as we know it now. True steel and road haulage had been returned to private ownership when Winston Churchill returned to power in 1951 but most industries had remained unchanged. Conservative principles and doctrines had borne little relation to Conservative practices.

For those of us active in St Andrews politics this was totally unsatisfactory. We saw no reason why the 'commanding heights of the economy' should not be better run by businessman than politicans. Indeed, one of the pamphlets produced by the St Andrews Tory Reform Group, of which I was a founder member, argued back in the 1960s for the sale of British Telecom, subsequently one of the most successful of all privatisations. We also called for the sale of council houses, in terms of sheer size the biggest of all privatisations.

We helped re-arouse the Conservative Party's interest in its long held principles. Edward Heath subsequently sold off Thomas Cook, the travel agents, and the Carlisle pubs, a legacy of the attempts to limit drinking amongt munitions workers in the First World War. These were minor changes for the better heavily overshadowed by his subsequent change of heart and for example the nationalisation of Rolls Royce.

But ideas have a momentum of their own and when Margaret Thatcher came to power in 1979 privatisation was back on the agenda. Initially on a small scale with enterprises such as Amersham International, an obscure radioactive medical equipment manufacturers that I suspect few people knew the Government owned. Another early one was the National Freight Corporation, a conglomerate of relatively unprofitable businesses which in another era might simply have been closed down but which now became the subject of a management buy-out. Highly successful it was to prove too, as the new worker-owners turned losses into profits and saw the value of their investment soar.

It was when it came to major industries, however, that the Government identified an unforeseen bonus underlying the application of its principles. The flotation of industries like British Telecom or British Gas, even the sale of the Government's holding in British Caledonian, brought in massive amounts of revenue to the Treasury. All at once privatisation ceased just to be a matter of principle but became a crucial part of helping balance the nation's books. The hunt was on to find more and more suitable subjects for sale to the public. That most powerful of Departments, the Treasury, was marching along with the market men.

For those brought up in the St Andrews tradition it seemed almost unbelievable as, one by one, activities we might only have dreamt about seeing removed from the pernicious influence of politicians and bureaucrats were identified for sale and sold.

In the majority of cases the new companies were created on a United Kingdom basis. Not only did it seem to make no sense to break up an organisation that was already operating successfully across the country as a whole but many of the new private companies were going to face competition on the world stage. Size would be important, was the conventional thinking.

When it came to electricity, however, the situation was quite different. Scotland for a long time had two boards, the South of Scotland Electricity Board and the North of Scotland Hydro-Electric Board, unlike in England where the generation, distribution and sale of electricity was supplies were handled by separate bodies. The entire system here in Scotland, from power station to domectic light bulb, was operated as an integrated system. Of course when it was appropriate the two Boards sold power to each other and to England. Supplies of Scotland's electricity played an important role in keeping England going during the miners' strike. But essentially the two Boards generated, distributed and sold their own electricity.

So when it came time to consider the Electricity Industry for privatisation it was easy to argue that Scotland should be treated apart from England. And so it was. A new structure was created based on the two existing boards but with the nuclear generators separated out to make a third element. Only the first two were to be privatised. The hard work of preparing this re-organisation fell to Ian Lang. I was at the time happily enjoying the freedom of the backbenches to watch others doing the hard work.

The actual privatisation, however, did not take place until after I had returned to the Scottish Office in 1990 where it fell to me, as Industry Minister, to see the sale successfully through under Ian Lang.

Unlike others, the Scottish Electricity privatisations were well priced. The shares initially went to a small premium then fell. This underpinned the credibility of the new companies' financial structure. Politically, it avoided the criticisms of quick profiteering which were levelled at some other privatisations.

In my 1990–1995 term as Industry Minister I was responsible

to Ian Lang for the Scottish New Towns and for Scottish Nuclear Ltd (SNL). The wind up of the New Towns was not strictly speaking privatisation, although many assets were transferred (sensibly) to the private sector. It was with great reluctance I agreed to undertake the preparations for the wind up of the New Towns, a proposition I had successfully resisted in my previous term as Industry Minister (1983–86). Since the public expenditure and planning benefits of the New Towns were something of a market bias, why did a free marketeer take that view? The reason was my belief that the key importance of the Scottish New Towns was not only their effort in Scottish economic, industrial and housing markets. I took the view that the five New Towns enhanced the competitiveness of Scotland plc in the international market for industrial investment. That was the market that mattered.

The New Towns' successful role in attracting mobile international investment often received criticism from older communities without the same range of industrial and environmental facilities. But the effective choice was often not between a Scottish New Town and an old town or city but between a Scottish New Town and another European country. But eventually the logic that New Towns could simply not for ever enjoy their special status won the day.

Working with Scottish Nuclear Ltd (SNL), a nationalised industry, was a pleasure. Under the leadership of James Hann and Robin Jeffrey the company completed a massive cultural shift. Under the former SSEB arrangements, nuclear staff had been almost exclusively production oriented. Now it had to be much more finance oriented and aware of the importance of public opinion. The key was not simply the high quality and direction of management, it was the prospect of privatisation. While civil servants retained their traditional and understandable caution, James and Robin were publicly enthusiastic, resulting in some unease in Government circles because of the past difficulties encountered with city opinion when the rest of the industry was privatised. I took the view very strongly that they were entirely entitled to express their opinions since eventual privatisation had not been ruled out by the Government.

During that period SNL launched a massive publicity campaign – advertisements, posters, visitor centres and touring exhibitions. They were absolutely correct to do so. Many people were ignorant and often misinformed about the nuclear industry. That campaign has been enormously successful.

It is a pity that the structure eventually adopted is not that advocated by SNL, which would have resulted in another major Scottish based company. But the industry will when privatised be able to raise its capital requirements in the market rather than being constrained by annual negotiations between the Scottish Office and the Treasury. As a nationalised industry SNL has been outside the 'block' arrangements.

As a backbencher I successfully piloted through the Commons a Private Bill on the Clyde Port Authority which was described by its opponents inaccurately as a privatisation measure. CPA was a trust port not a nationalised industry. The Bill – to give CPA normal company status – which involved a great deal of work to organise parliamentary supporters, passed its various stages in the Commons with substantial majorities. To everyone's extreme irritation it failed to pass the Lords not because of lack of support but because of obscure drafting technicalities. However, as in the case of the Licensing Amendment Bill, the battle may have been lost but the war was won. The Government subsequently introduced enabling legislation under which Clydeport, among many others, has been able to move successfully into the normal company sector.

Privatisation is at its best when, as in the case of most of the early measures, the resulting company operates in a competitive environment, so safeguarding the consumers' interests. The Scottish Bus Group is an outstanding example.

The general market interest and the Scottish interest tend to coincide when large British industries are being privatised – ie to break them up.

That was regrettably not achieved with steel but was with coal. Those with a real interest and knowledge in the Scottish coalfield – such as Campbell Christie, Eric Clarke, Ross Harper and John Mackay (Lord Mackay of Ardbrecknish) all worked hard and successfully for it to be separately privatised.

The answer to the problems of privatising natural monopolies or near monopolies is to set up regulatory mechanisms such as OFWAT, OFTEL and so on. But it is no coincidence that the only privatisation yet to show clear benefits to the consumer is that of the English water companies. The Government is now introducing measures to force competition between the companies for industrial users. It will have to move further down that road for a satisfactory structure to emerge.

The pre-privatisation structure of water and sewage in England and Wales did however lend itself reasonably well to moving it into the private sector, leaving aside the natural monopoly problem.

The position in Scotland was historically and radically different. The debate which took place before and during the passage of the Local Government Reform Bill was not started because of a desire to privatise water and sewerage in Scotland. It was an inevitable consequence of local government reorganisation. Naturally in consultation, privatisation was mentioned as one of a wide range of options. But, even leaving aside public opinion, the natural monopoly, organisational and financial problems would have been immense and there was of course simply no need to contemplate seriously such a course – nor any need to contemplate it in the future. The new structure meets monopoly problems, with the Consumers' Council and ultimately central government policy control. And it meets the need to raise external capital to fund investment, notably through build, own and operate schemes.

The involvement of private finance is not only desirable, it is essential. Everyone, naturally enough talks of water. But the main problem is sewerage (I suppose a campaign entitled Hands off Scotland's Sewage would not have had the same ring to it). It is sewerage which is the main spender both now and in the future, when everyone agrees around £5billion will be required to be invested to meet European Union directives.

The financing problems for the Scottish Office derives directly from the Barnett rules. As explained elsewhere, these mean that the Scottish Office automatically receives 10.66% of any change in the expenditure of a comparable English Department. But in England, water and sewerage are privatised. There is no comparable programme. Putting it at its simplest, 10.66% of zero is zero. Hence there are only three sources of revenue for additional capital expenditure – the industry itself through charges, switching money from other Scottish programmes such as Health, or the private sector. The first is difficult beyond a limited extent, the second would obviously cause very serious problems for other public expenditure programmes.

In the long term however there is an exciting prospect for the Scottish water and sewerage boards. Scotland has a surplus of good clean water, whereas parts of England have water shortages that will become steadily worse. Water in Scotland can be exported as long as it is surplus to our own requirements. To do that on a significant and continuing scale would require massive investment running into billions. A number of studies have been successfully undertaken. It is an opportunity for the future. But it is an opportunity which one day it will be sensible to grasp.

## CHAPTER 18

# THE WAY AHEAD

Gerald Warner introduces his authoritive history of the Scottish Tory Party by recalling the words of Henry Cockburn in 1832 – "The regeneration of Scotland is now secured. The Tory Party, as such, is extinguished." All parties have peaks and troughs. The Scottish Tories have certainly had their share of the lows.

For a party describing itself as Conservative, traditional institutions in our Constitution are to be improved and to be adjusted to circumstances but treated with care. So the recent changes, for example to the Scottish Grand Committee, introduced particularly by Ian Lang and Michael Forsyth, are essentially Conservative changes.

Scottish Tories opposed the 1707 Treaty of Union since they

were Jacobites, but after some time accepted the Union as an accomplished fact and worked to improve it. The first identifable Scottish Tory slogan may have been No Union, but to defend the Union now is historically consistent.

Were Labour to win the next General Election and success-fully introduce a Scottish Parliament – and neither proposition is by any means certain – the Conservative and Unionist Party would be confronted by a challenge similar to that faced by their eighteenth century predecessors – how does a party which believes in the continuity of the constitutional fabric react to a violent and unwelcome change to that constitution?

Naturally it is not a question yet raised since all our energies are directed to winning the election and so defeating Labour's devolution plans. To discuss it here is not to undermine those efforts but hopefully to assist them by highlighting some of the dangers in the Opposition's current proposals, to which scant attention has been paid.

Despite Unionist efforts, should a Scottish Parliament be set up, Tories would very soon be required to answer a simple question – what would a subsequent Conservative Government's policy towards it be?

In theory, the choice would be three way:

(1) to abolish it;
(2) to make it workable;
(3) to agree full independence.

Abolition would be logical. It would be a new, not revitalised part of the constitution. Vague proposals about somehow entrenching the existence of a Scottish Parliament or Assembly are wholly misleading. A United Kingdom Parliament cannot bind its successor. Also, central Government would hold most of the purse strings. It would be possible fairly simply to take the necessary measures to have expenditure per head financed by the Exchequer, brought immediately into line with that in England and Wales. Or for that matter lower as the quid pro quo for the Tartan Tax-raising capacity in order to retain control of the total Public Sector Borrowing Requirement.

Such financial measures would probably be necessary for Option 2 (acceptance) but might also result in a climate of opinion in which the advantages to Scotland of a return to the Union became self-evident. Abolition of Labour-introduced Scottish devolution by a subsequent Conservative and Unionist Government would be feasible. It would be simple, since the constitution would be returned to the present arrangements. Whether it would be popular would depend on circumstances, notably how far the unworkability of the present proposals had become apparent – north and south of the border.

Option 2 – announcing future Conservative policy to make a Scottish Parliament work – has no logical merit. But it would be in line with the traditional Conservative philosophy of endeavouring to improve what is in place. It is often maintained that Britain has an unwritten constitution. Although of course we do not have a written constitution in the American sense, strictly speaking this is not accurate. One very considerable advantage of the British constitution is that it is much more flexible than other countries. There is in addition a considerable willingness, especially among the English, to muddle through, to make the best of a bad job. No Conservative would willingly make an existing institution unworkable. A package which would be a marked improvement on the present proposals could be devised. A very sharp reduction in the number of Scottish MPs at Westminster is obvious. That would not answer the famous West Lothian question but would reduce to a limited extent the intensity of the difficulty. As suggested above, public expenditure changes would be required.

Liberal Democrats answer the difficulties of unilateral devolution by moving down the federalist route. That was an approach tried but effectively abandoned by the Labour Party, now in the curious position of promising referendums for local government changes in England but not for their much trumpeted Scottish devolution proposals. It is not a possible approach for Conservatives. Because a problem exists in one part of the Union is no basis for fundamental change elsewhere – especially as there is almost no evidence of any deep desire in England to move down a federal route.

Given that unilateral devolution is a recipe for certain and continuing conflict between Edinburgh and London – a one way street for the SNP – the difficulty of Option 2 becomes apparent. Conservatives would be trying to make the unworkable work.

That leaves the apparently unthinkable, Option 3. A swift move from devolution to separation might occur in any event, even during the next Parliament. The Labour Party appear not to have even considered the possibilities. In mid term (when elections to a devolved body would be held) all Governments tend to be unpopular. What would happen if the elections to the devolved Parliament returned, in an extreme case, an SNP majority or, more likely, a majority of SNP and Conservative members? In the extreme case the SNP would demand immediate, full independence.

For the Conservative and Unionist Party the breakup of the Union would be an appalling wrench. Politics is by no means only about logic and economics and the provision of public services. It is about history, traditions and emotions. John Major spoke for the entire party when he told a Conservative conference, speaking on devolution,

> My commitment to the Union is total. It's not just a political commitment – it's emotional as well. And I'm not ashamed of that.
>
> I feel, with every fibre of my being, that the result of this folly would be dismemberment of the United Kingdom.

Forecasting in politics is more hazardous and difficult than ever. But what an irony it would be if a Unionist party had to face the irreparable breakdown of the Union following devolution and had to conclude that Option 3 – the separation of Scotland from the remainder of the United Kingdom – was the only sensible policy.

Curiously enough, in the long term the Conservatives both north and south of the border would, in purely partisan terms, almost certainly benefit from such a move. The party advantage in England is obvious. Without Labour's Scottish majority to contend with the Conservatives would have a much higher chance of obtaining control at Westminster.

Scotland may be more collectivist than England, but there is little evidence the electorate are fundamentally left wing. Since the Unionists were returned in 1955 with over 50% of the popular vote (never achieved by Labour) Scottish Tories have suffered from being identified as an English party. That the charge is totally without foundation is not the point. People believe it. Parties of the centre right are historically seen as patriotic – associated with people's deep political customs and beliefs.

In Scotland the Tories, after the trauma of a complete breakdown of the Union, would be able to gain the natural centre right vote. There is no reason to believe free market ideas would not prosper in the land of Adam Smith. Is such a constitutional and political catalyst desirable? Of course not. But such an outcome would be entirely the Labour Party's own fault.

The Conservative Party will fight hard for its beliefs and principles. Earlier chapters discussed both principles and detailed political action. The free market philosophy, pamphleteering and political action at St Andrews represented an unusual set of circumstances. But there is a lesson to be drawn from that early experience. Party workers are volunteers. They need to be blessed with firm beliefs so that they reach through hard work to grass roots Conservatives and possible Conservative voters.

It has not been the purpose of this book to examine party organisation. In 1979 the East Renfrewshire campaign had a professional agent, while in the subsequent three elections the agent has been the former Regional Councillor, Peter Edmondson, a friend of immense political knowledge and shrewdness. My 1992 Campaign Director was Jackson Carlaw whose outstanding campaigning flair is certain to continue to be of immense value to Chairman Sir Michael Hirst and to the party.

However, in my experience it has been all too easy down the years for some in the Tory Party to blame the Central Office team

– a convenient scapegoat. My first speech to a Scottish Conservative and Unionist Conference (1968) was a strong defence of the
Scottish Central Office. That was motivated by a concern that the
'It's all the fault of Central Office' sentiment was a damaging cop-
out. Fortunately at present, the indomitable enthusiasm and sheer
slog of Micky Hirst and his team will prevent any such tendencies.

They and the Conservative and Unionist Party face a real
challenge to make it five wins in a row against a modernised
Labour Party, which has on policy (except the constitution)
adopted a new version of the historic model of the three wise
monkeys – hear no policy, see no policy, but above all say no
policy. That political challenge has paradoxically been made
tougher by the victories of market economy principles.

The ditching of Labour's Clause 4 may not have meant much
in practice – nobody I met ever really believed a Labour
Government would nationalise everything in sight – but it was
symbolic.

The market men led politically by one remarkable woman
have triumphed. The ratchet is now the other way. For so long it
appeared that Labour Governments would move Britain towards
collectivism and Conservatives would not be able to fundamentally reverse the tide. No longer. The market revolution is in place
and is in most respects irreversible. Does that mean market
economy thinkers have little more to say? Far from it. The reasons
are both political and economic.

Politically, in our complex, sophisticated and democratic
society the pace of social and economic change is without
precedent. New problems are constantly brought to the attention
of the political process. Harold MacMillan, when Prime Minister,
was once asked by a new MP what he feared most in Government.
"Events, dear boy, events," the old magician replied.

Events in politics, require responses. As I argued earlier,
given a perceived problem the political system is placed under
immediate pressure to respond in one or other of two ways. It can
alter public expenditure or it can regulate. The demands are always
– "but what is the Government going to do?" Democratic

governments must fashion coherent responses.

So there will be continuing pressure, irrespective of party, on the Government of the day to respond to pressures through increasing both public expenditure and regulation. Those pressures may in future sometimes be entirely sensible. A market economy requires a framework of regulation on such matters as health, safety and the avoidance of monopoly or anti-competitive practices. Indeed, weak government can positively damage not only consumers and the economy but the whole case for private enterprise – as set out in the comments on privatisation earlier. Problems will always arise – such as those created by the English water companies. It will be up to the proponents of market forces to be at the forefront of finding answers.

In policy area after area, major questions remain to be answered. To mention only a few – What is the scope for motorway tolling and indeed for road pricing in badly congested areas such as London and Edinburgh? How far can the polluter pays principle be applied to environmental problems? Could private prisons, currently experimental, be widely and sensibly applied? For individuals, elderly relatives and their care are often the most important single worry. So what is the balance between private provision and the safety net of the state? Those who save are notably disheartened when their sacrifices appear pointless because those who have not done so receive identical provision in old age. Our ageing population is a success story – a tribute to rising living standards and the National Health Service. But it is also a social and public expenditure time bomb. There will have to answers.

Nor can the smaller issues be ignored – part of the success of the protagonists of market principles has been precisely that concentration on specifics – micro economy rather than macro. The Forestry Commission (a Scottish Office responsibility) and the Private Finance Initiative are only two examples.

As pointed out earlier Europe will be the great political issue of the future. The broad market approach may have won the day in the United Kingdom, but that is by no means necessarily the case in the European Union. In one sense that is surprising. The founding fathers saw themselves as establishing a Common Market. A Common Market was what we all thought we were joining when we voted in the 1975 Referendum.

Supporters of market principles should therefore be enthusiastic pro-Europeans. Or should they? It depends on the kind of Europe we mean. The Single Market as such is highly desirable. Brussels' competition policy – a level playing field on state aid is highly desirable. It is particularly important for an economy such as Scotland's which depends relatively heavily on regional industrial incentives and on inward investment. On a number of inward investment cases in which I was involved, we deeply suspected the incentive packages being offered by competitors. State aid to airlines by continental countries, under various guises, remains a gross distortion and affront to the principles of the Treaty of Rome. These and similar problems will require to be rigorously addressed. The answer is more effective policing power for Brussels not less.

But fundamentally and seriously central control remains the trend of European policy. The drift is unquestionably in a steadily regulatory direction. Other than in the business community most European leaders appear not to appreciate the dangers of a heavily regulated and controlled European industry. It is very simply that European business will lose world market share, particularly to the much less regulated 'Asian Tigers'. That in turn could lead to loud and well organised calls for a more protectionist Europe (not that the slogan would be protectionism of course).

All this suggests an urgent need for those who believe in the kind of Europe originally envisaged to join intellectual and political forces. Needless centralism and regulations are as much against the interests of Italians or Danes as they are against ours.

For those who believe in individual choice, economic freedom, private enterprise, competition and the dynamism of market economies, the main challenge has now moved. The challenge is what kind of Europe we shall have in ten years' time and beyond.

## INDEX